For almost three decades Mark Stephens has helped thousands change their lives. In 1990 Mark discovered he had cancer and was given a possible six months to live with a rapidly growing lymphoma. He had to utilise everything he had learned to overcome the challenge he faced.

Twenty years later and with a clean bill of health he continues to travel the country and inspire people to transform their own lives for the better through his seminars, keynote speeches and groundbreaking hypnosis and motivation programs.

Mark is a ju-jutsu black belt, tai chi teacher, chi kung teacher, shiatzu practitioner, master practitioner and trainer of hypnosis, internationally accredited trainer of neurolinguistic programming, accredited trainer of Time Line Therapy™ and author of Think Slim.

Think Quit

Smoke-free forever

Mark Stephens

ARENA
ALLEN&UNWIN

This book is not intended to replace the advice of a doctor or trained medical professional. If you suffer from any mental condition, psychological disorder or are currently on medication for such disorders, please seek the advice of your doctor before commencing this or any other smoking cessation program.

First published in 2010

Arena Books, an imprint of
Allen & Unwin
83 Alexander Street
Crows Nest NSW 2065
Australia
Phone: (61 2) 8425 0100
Fax: (61 2) 9906 2218
Email: info@allenandunwin.com
Web: www.allenandunwin.com

Cataloguing-in-Publication details are available
from the National Library of Australia
www.librariesaustralia.nla.gov.au

ISBN 978 1 74237 314 0

Set in 11.5/14 pt Joanna MT by Midland Typesetters, Australia
Printed in Australia by McPherson's Printing Group

10 9 8 7 6 5 4 3 2 1

To those who have struggled and tried,
yet still are determined to be smoke-free,
this book is for you.

CONTENTS

ACKNOWLEDGEMENTS

To my best friend and gorgeous wife Linda, whose input and work ethic keep the wheels turning every step of the way. I am forever grateful for your boundless, unconditional love, for your encouragement and for the feedback that keeps it real.

To Velvet, my other best friend, thank you for curling up at my feet and keeping them warm during those early mornings and late nights typing away. Thank you for your patience in waiting to go for walks and for giving Linda and me 12 years of pure love and so much joy.

Special thanks go to Lynn Thomas (who also happens to be my loving Mum) for the tireless transcribing of the Think Quit audio program. If she said it once, she said it a thousand times: 'If you were meant to smoke you'd have a chimney out the top of your head.' You taught me as a child to believe in myself and help others. This has been invaluable and shaped my life.

To Tad James, who encourages, motivates and educates in a way nobody else can. Thank you for the years of invaluable instruction, training and support.

To Louise Thurtell, my publisher, your encouragement and the belief that this book could help so many people has made this a reality. Thank you for believing in me so I could believe in others enough for them to believe in themselves.

To the countless clients who over the years have given me the feedback that has allowed me to adjust and develop Think Quit so it could evolve to where it is today. Thank you for your input, your accomplishments and your commitment to changing your life and being smoke-free. Your success has been, and continues to be, my inspiration and motivation.

TESTIMONIALS FROM THOSE WHO HAVE QUIT SMOKING WITH *THINK QUIT*

I started smoking 38 years ago when I was 17 years of age. On average I'd be smoking a pack to a pack and a half a day. I had tried to quit lots of times with no success. I went through terrible cravings. It was just awful—gut-wrenching cravings is the only way you could describe it. My husband actually went to the shops and bought me cigarettes and said: 'Here Pam, smoke them; I can't live with you—no one can.'

I think with the Think Quit program, because you do the seven days first, you are so prepared. I was ready for the cravings, I was expecting cravings, but they were nowhere nearly as bad as any of the cravings that I had experienced in the past. Compared to other methods, with Think Quit I was so prepared, I was ready. I had my alternatives there if I had a craving. I knew what I was going to do. I enjoy the ease of having that little MP4 player that you can just take anywhere with you. The craving-busting sessions were very, very good. You can do it on the spot. Instead of having a cigarette, it's just a flick of the switch, put the earphones in, that's it, craving gone. I will never, ever smoke again. And I say that with confidence. I am just a different person; my health is better, my attitude's better, my whole family are proud of me. I have been smoking all those years, and why? I have been smoke-free for almost three years now and I will never smoke again.

—Pam Gill, *Gold Coast*

After smoking for more than 20 years I've tried just about every stop-smoking technique known to man. The thing I liked most about the Think Quit program was that the meditation and hypnosis sessions were fantastic. I felt really calm throughout the process. Normally, when you give up smoking there's the anxiety of having no back-up, you're there alone living through the experience, whereas with Think Quit I felt that I had something to go back to. In terms of the preparation, I found the seven-day diary quite simple and I can really see now, looking back, how important keeping that diary is. My main triggers for smoking actually came out of the seven-day diary that I kept and it was really fascinating.

By the time Q-Day comes around you are totally prepared and have done all the foundation to be ready for that moment when you stop. I had nine smoking triggers, and identifying them and going back to the origin of each trigger was just brilliant. It was a great release of whatever you connected to that trigger. And you could apply that to any aspect of your life. Just after I quit I went on a conference which I was a little bit nervous about as people around me were smoking but at no point did I feel like having a cigarette—it was fantastic. Think Quit is a very comprehensive concept and you are actually given a great deal of support. I feel much better about myself now that I don't smoke. It has been well over two years since I have touched a cigarette. I now have control over something that had controlled me for so long. Think Quit is fantastic.

—Paul Clarke, Sydney

I always said I'd give it up when I was 50. I reached 50 and I was actually on patches and gum and I was still smoking. I was short of breath, I couldn't exercise and I was getting colds more often. I have not touched a cigarette now for two and a half years. I don't even think about it. Think Quit rewires your brain. It not only deals with the physical addiction, it deals with the mental stress of giving up smoking as well. I just feel I'm a non-smoker and I know I will never touch another cigarette again. My son smokes at home and other people around me smoke but I am not tempted to smoke. Twice I had given up, and this time it's different because now I feel like a non-smoker. If you are thinking of stopping, stop straight away, don't waste any more money, don't ruin your life any longer, don't let your health deteriorate any more than it already has. *Think Quit* makes stopping easy.

—Suzanne Martin, Sydney

Firstly I would like to say that 'I AM NOW A NON-SMOKER'. I love saying that. Thank you so much for changing my life; I really thought I would never get rid of that foul habit. I had tried a lot of things in the past and it never worked—even falling pregnant with my daughter Cleo didn't help me quit, and I swore I was going to give it up but it had a such a hold on me!! Now I know differently and that's thanks to you. I really could sit here all day and all night thanking you. The gift that you have given us at such a small price is really priceless because you have given us our life back, and I thank you. My daughter, my partner and my family also thank you.

—Bec

I started smoking to 'look cool' early in my teens. When I started university I was smoking a packet a day. I then started my 'I should quit' phase, which lasted about ten years! In this ten-year period, I would smoke anywhere from one to 20 cigarettes a day. I can't even count how often I tried to quit.

Never in that time did I think of myself as a non-smoker. I would hold a cigarette, inhale unlit cigarettes, go out with the smokers when they were on their break. I would tell myself it was disgusting and dirty but the cravings never ended. Then I would have just one and then one more and then I'd be back smoking. I would blame having a stressful job, then tell myself I enjoyed smoking or tell myself it would keep me slim, and then tell myself it was OK and the diseases would never happen to me.

Then along came Mark Stephens, claiming he had the cure. I was getting sick of the sore throat, the bad breath, the smelly fingers and the wasted gym membership because I couldn't keep up in an aerobics class. I was desperate, even though I didn't really admit it at the time.

The Think Quit program was so easy to follow. The program advises you to continue smoking for the first week—I couldn't even do that. The smoking lasted five days out of the seven, and I had to stop because I was getting physically ill. By the end of the seven days I could not believe I had smoked for 15 years. For the first time in 15 years, I was a non-smoker. When people asked, the answer was 'I don't smoke'. This is the best investment I have ever made for me, by me. I would pay tenfold to achieve success like this again. Almost 12 months after the program, I am saying, without a hesitation in my mind, I will never smoke again. Ever!

—Silvia Polakovic, Victoria

Tomorrow will be 60 days since I stopped smoking, and it just seems to get easier as I find my automatic smoking triggers are now automatically replaced with healthy alternatives. My doctor is really impressed with the change in my breathing and blood pressure. The strains on my heart have eased considerably and although I will still require a heart transplant due to the damage done by my immune system, there is now more time to find a donor heart as my heart is not under as much strain.

Quitting has been a lot easier than I first thought, but this time I was determined to quit. I just needed some professional help to get over the hurdles that I have always stumbled at. Thank you so much for that. There are so many others who just need to know that this does work.

My ex-wife was in awe and disbelief when I sent her an email today. She was thrilled for me. (And wished you had been around 30 years ago.)

—Colin Wragg, Victoria

INTRODUCTION

Welcome to the Think Quit program, and congratulations for making the decision to eliminate cigarettes from your life.

This book, with your bonus MP3 audio sessions, holds the key to your success in becoming smoke-free forever and creating the healthy future you deserve. You will discover in this book the tips and strategies that will help you to make the transition to being smoke-free. You are going to find this whole process easier than you thought because Think Quit takes a holistic approach to becoming smoke-free. By holistic I mean we will tackle the physical challenges related to eliminating the smoking habit as well as any mental struggles.

In the past, you may have attempted to quit smoking and lasted a day, a week or even longer. Unfortunately, for some reason you started smoking again—otherwise you wouldn't be reading this right now.

Over the years, I have worked with clients on a variety of issues ranging from phobias and overcoming anxiety to pain control, weight loss and sleep problems. When working in a one-on-one consultation with a client for smoking cessation, I use a wide variety of methods to help the client overcome all the challenges that relate to stopping smoking. Because we are not in a face-to-face therapy session here, I have adapted these techniques and exercises in a way that will allow you to follow these techniques and exercises as you read through the book.

There is no magic bullet approach to quitting, no one-method cure that works for every single smoker. As you practise the different exercises found in this book, bear in mind that you will discover what works best for you when it comes to stopping smoking.

People with whom I've worked successfully had previously tried to stop smoking using various methods, including patches, gum, cold turkey, doctor-prescribed medications, laser therapy, acupuncture and hypnosis.

I would like you to disregard the past. Forget about failed attempts and approach the Think Quit program with a can-do attitude. To make sure you succeed, this book is packed with dozens of life-changing strategies so you will be able to stop smoking easily. One page at a time, you will learn what it takes to kick the nicotine addiction and the smoking habit permanently. You will be able to create the transformations in your life that you desire. As you carefully read through every page, you will discover your own personal secret key to being smoke-free.

In Think Quit, you will learn how to eliminate the triggers that have kept the old habit alive. You will be told exactly how to crush the belief that you need to smoke as you are taken through the program step by step. You will be shown how to replace the old, poisonous nicotine habit with new, positive, healthy and invigorating habits.

This will work.

This book covers in detail the strategies needed to become smoke-free and remain that way. You will be given all the tools you need to take total control of your life.

Have faith in the Think Quit program. And even more import-antly, believe in yourself. You have within you all the resources to succeed. It will be my job via this book and the MP3 downloads (see page 8 for details on these) to reprogram your mind for success and to tap into those resources, allowing you to create the healthy future you deserve.

I look forward to being your motivational support person, your mind coach and your hypnotherapist via this book and your bonus download sessions.

Be sure to let me know about your successful achievement!

Yours in health and a longer—much longer—smoke-free life.

Mark Stephens

HOW THE PROGRAM WORKS

Think Quit is divided into three parts. Part I covers the reasons why you continue smoking and looks at why, in the past, you may have had difficulty stopping. This section of the book also gives general information about smoking, including the health dangers of continuing to smoke and the benefits of stopping. You will also discover why it is easier to quit than you might think.

The majority of smokers seem to have a pretty tight grip on their smoking problem. The habit has been reinforced both mentally and physically, over and over. The first part of this book is very important, as it helps you to loosen the grip you may have on the problem. Part I helps prepare you for the Seven-Day Preparation Program. As you read through this section, you will understand more about the addiction and how you can and will overcome the smoking trap.

Part II is your Seven-Day Preparation Program. This section is aimed at preparing you both mentally and physically by providing you with all the tools and strategies you will need to become permanently smoke-free. Each day you will learn simple relaxation techniques, breathing exercises and mental strategies in preparation for your Quit Day, referred to as 'Q-Day'. Each day you will reinforce earlier exercises while learning new exercises and stop-smoking strategies. You will also fill in your seven-day smoking diary, which is at the back of the book in Part III. It is very important that you fill in the smoking diary, as this helps to bring into your conscious awareness those things which may have been largely outside of your awareness. Smoking is not just one habit. The smoking habit is actually multi-layered and includes taking a cigarette from the pack or rolling one up if you smoke rollies, flicking a lighter switch or striking a match then watching the flame when you light up, holding something between your fingers, and putting something in your mouth. All these triggers could be described as 'sub-habits' of the smoking addiction. Habits are largely unconscious, so filling in your diary helps you to be fully aware of your smoking triggers and the state of mind associated with each trigger. By filling in the diary, you are also making a commitment to yourself to stop once and for all. A half-hearted approach will give you little result. It is time to get serious and stop smoking.

You will find important phrases repeated a number of times. In a one-on-one hypnosis session, the phrase 'You are now smoke-free' may be repeated dozens of times. These phrases are hypnotic suggestions or powerful statements that you will use to change your mindset. As you read these suggestions to yourself, day by day you will replace the old, negative self-talk with new, positive self-talk.

It is important not to skip any exercises. As you go through each exercise and strategy, you will get a feeling for what works best for you. One relaxation technique or breathing exercise may suit you more than others, so it is up to you to work out which of them will work best for you. In effect, you will be customising the program to suit yourself.

Day by day throughout Part II, you will be breaking down the old patterns, habits and mindset that have held you prisoner. Before commencing the Seven-Day Preparation Program, you will need to set the date for your Q-Day, which is the day after your seven days of preparation. In effect, everything you do will lead you towards the crucial eighth day, Q-Day. This is the day when you will wake up and not touch another cigarette. During the Seven-Day Preparation Program you will continue to smoke while preparing yourself to be smoke-free.

How much time do you need?

Some people choose to stop smoking during their annual holidays or take a week off to stop. Others time Q-Day so that it falls late in the week, allowing them the weekend to get through the first couple of days. If you can take Q-Day off, making it a Friday, that may also help. Let me say here, though, that many people who have used the Think Quit program have had few to no cravings, and this may be your experience. It all boils down to being committed, changing your mindset and being prepared. Appreciating that most people have busy lifestyles, I have kept all the relaxation techniques and exercises as simple as possible.

As busy as you are, you need to make this an important step and not treat it as 'just reading a book'. Take several minutes a few times each day to practise the exercises and you will make life so much easier on yourself when you reach Q-Day. In some instances, clients have turned the Seven-Day Preparation Program into eight or nine days; if you feel you need an extra couple of days to be totally prepared, that is OK; however, I would not put it off much longer than two or three days. On the other hand, I have had people stop smoking on Day 3 or 4 of the preparation program. This is risky if you have not completed all the exercises, and I would recommend you follow the seven days as outlined to give yourself the greatest chance of success. If you are totally repulsed by cigarettes on Day 4 or 5, that is a good thing. Simply record in your diary when you smoked and what the trigger was for smoking. You may decide to light up and put the cigarette straight out, or you may simply feel like cutting down the number of cigarettes you smoke dramatically during the last day or two of the seven-day preparation. You may choose to smoke half of each cigarette towards the end of the week. The most important thing is that for the seven days you follow all the exercises and all of the self-hypnosis sessions so you can become smoke-free.

If you feel you need additional support, check the resources available, such as the Think Quit MP4 player or other support CDs, in the resource section on pages 243–6.

Self-hypnosis sessions

The Seven-Day Preparation Program contains several self-hypnosis sessions. There are a number of different ways to do these:

1. Read them to yourself silently or out loud. While reading, do your best to imagine what is being described. Take your time and read each script slowly, as this will give your mind time to paint the pictures and let the messages sink in. If you like particular sessions, repeat these a number of times to increase the benefits and reinforce the message.
2. Ask somebody else to read them to you. Make sure the person reads the script in a calm, relaxed tone with lots of pauses. You may also like to have relaxing music playing in the background.
3. The Think Quit MP4 program has dozens of motivation and hypnosis sessions along with video coaching sessions. If you feel you need the additional support of the Think Quit pocket therapist, check out the resource section at the back of the book or visit www.thinkquit.com.au.

Bonus MP3 downloads

As the owner of this book, you will also have access to three bonus MP3 download hypnosis sessions from the Think Quit program. You will need to visit www.thinkquit.com.au to download your bonus sessions. Session 1 is a relaxation session that you can listen to during your Seven-Day Preparation Program as well as once you have stopped smoking. Session 2 is a hypnosis session to help you change your mindset about smoking and can be listened to the night before Q-Day. Session 3 is the main Q-Day stop-smoking hypnosis session and is to be listened to first thing on Q-Day and repeatedly as needed during the first three to four weeks. Some people listen to this session once and that is enough. Others listen to the session every morning and every night to reinforce the positive suggestions. The three downloads are free with this book.

Downloading your bonus hypnosis sessions

Step 1: Visit **www.thinkquit.com.au**.

Step 2: Click on the Think Quit: Smoke-free forever book image.

Step 3: Click on BONUS DOWNLOAD.

Step 4: Type in the user name 'thinkquit' as one word (lower case).

Step 5: Type in the password: AU77sffms.

Step 6: Follow download instructions.

Understanding the mental triggers

While there are many approaches to stopping smoking, you will find the beauty of this program is that, step by step over seven days, you will tackle the mental aspect of smoking. You will totally prepare yourself to break free once and for all from the nicotine prison. For the first time, you will get to the causes of smoking and tackle all the triggers that have kept you hooked for so long.

Unfortunately, while benefiting some people, many methods of quitting do little to uncover the underlying issues of why people smoke. If you are on patches or gum but do little to disconnect the triggers that keep you smoking, then you face an uphill battle. Think Quit helps you tackle every challenge from stress to boredom and from the physical cravings to the mental. This book has been based on one-on-one sessions, stop-smoking seminars and the Think Quit MP4 audio and video program. Success awaits you.

PART I | Change your mind, change your life

1 | THE *THINK QUIT* MINDSET

If I could wave a magic wand over you and instantly stop you from smoking, for how long would you want to be smoke-free? A day, a week, a year? When asked this question, most clients say they want to be smoke-free forever. They never want to touch another cigarette again. I have never had a client say they would like to stop smoking for three years and start again. In fact, most people I talk to say they wish they had never started.

Around five years ago, I worked with a high-profile public figure; we'll call her Jenny to protect her identity. Jenny had been smoking for more than 25 years and claimed she had tried every method known to mankind to stop. The longest Jenny claimed to have stopped smoking for was four months. She had lost count of the number of times she had stopped for three days: the first two days seemed OK, but after that Jenny would lose it and light up that one cigarette that would ruin her best intentions.

Escape was easy, Jenny explained, but staying free was what had eluded her all these years. Jenny also told me that she had read somewhere that it takes on average seven attempts to finally quit. 'If that is the case, I am so ready to stop it is not funny,' Jenny stated.

In the end, Jenny said she would not even bother to throw out her cigarettes each time she stopped because she knew she would not be able to last more than a few days.

'I know how bad it is for me. I know I'm poisoning myself and it makes me feel weak that I can't stop,' said Jenny, sounding overwhelmed.

I asked myself what it was that Jenny needed to know that would allow her to make the greatest possible change and become smoke-free. How could we disconnect all the triggers and associations that had been reinforced thousands of times? What would motivate her to stay smoke-free and never touch another cigarette? What decision did Jenny need to make that would allow her to break free from the nicotine prison after so many failed attempts? What action would then be needed to follow through to bring about the desired outcome?

What she needed was strong motivation followed by massive action.

I asked Jenny to write me a list of all the things she didn't like about cigarettes. Here is part of the list Jenny came up with:

- Running out of puff from just walking up a flight of steps.
- Constant colds, and bronchitis that is hard to kick.
- Excessive coughing and phlegm.
- Ashtray taste in the mouth.
- Ageing skin and wrinkles around my mouth.
- Smoking to stay slim with the fear of putting on weight if I stop.
- Nicotine-stained fingers.
- Racing out late at night like a drug addict to buy cigarettes.
- Not being able to taste or smell things like flowers or meals very well.
- Yellowing teeth.
- Having to hide when smoking.
- Fear and anxiety over ending up with a serious illness.

Now that I knew what Jenny didn't want, I needed to find out what she *did* want.

Here's the thing: some people are motivated by what is known as 'away from' or 'negative' motivations. These are all the things you *don't* want. Other people are motivated by 'toward' or 'positive' motivations. Ask yourself: What do you want? What is the positive outcome you are seeking? And then there is a third group of people who are motivated by a mix of both negative and positive motivations. As your mind coach, I would normally ask you a series of questions and then customise the session and language used in a way that fits in with your exact needs and your model of the world.

Throughout the book, I have used a mix of techniques— both negative and positive in motivation—that will, somewhere along the way, start to make sense to you. At some point, the penny will drop. Some parts of the book may make more sense to you than other parts. Certain elements of what you read and learn will click with you. When you come across things that do not relate to you, feel free to discard those bits of information as you take on board the elements that make the most sense.

In the following pages, we will lay the foundations for you to be in control of your life and stay smoke-free forever.

Life as a non-smoker is only a matter of days away.

You will discover that Think Quit is like nothing you have ever done before.

It is time to stop smoking

Let me tell you why the Think Quit program is different from any other program or smoking-cessation tool, and why you will succeed. As you will discover throughout this program, smoking is not only a physical addiction but a mental addiction as well. Because of this, we will be taking a mind/body approach.

The Think Quit program combines the best of ancient healing methods with the latest mind-changing strategies to ensure you succeed. With each passing day, your health will improve. It is time to take back your life and your health. Think Quit makes stopping easy, even when all else has failed.

The following will lay the foundations for you to be a non-smoker and stay smoke-free. Bear in mind that this is a do-it-yourself program. No one will be there holding a gun to your head. But if you have had your head in the sand, it is time to take it out.

There are three important things you need to ask yourself: Am I truly ready to stop smoking? Am I serious about making this work? Am I 100 per cent committed to being smoke-free? If you answered yes to these three questions, you will be able to stop smoking easily.

Research has shown that people who are seriously ready and are doing it for themselves have a high success rate. However, it is very important to have a plan to follow.

By reading the following chapters, and committing yourself to the Seven-Day Preparation Program, you will be thoroughly prepared when you get to Q-Day. If smoking is so hard to stop, why are half the people who ever smoked now non-smokers? Let me tell you why. They were ready to stop! They did not want to be one of the almost five million people who die worldwide every year from smoking-related illnesses.

The fact that you are reading this book means you have made the decision to be smoke-free, to be a non-smoker, to stop smoking forever. You may already have tried to quit, you may have had short-term success—even long-term success—or you may have had no success at all, but that is in the past and it is time to let go of the past.

People smoke for many reasons: maybe you smoke to reduce stress or to socialise. Some people smoke out of habit. Smoking is a part of doing something else. Maybe you associate finishing a meal with having a cigarette. Maybe you think coffee or alcohol tastes better when you're having a cigarette. Maybe when you get into the car or when you wake up in the morning you want a cigarette—the list goes on and on.

The one thing that almost every smoker has in common is that they smoke because of the highly addictive nature of nicotine and the need to satisfy the craving caused by nicotine. Smokers habitually respond to stress by automatically lighting up.

As you change your mind, you change your life. Once you become a non-smoker, you will be taking control of your life. It will be obvious to you at the moment that smoking and nicotine control you, but you are about to change that and control the habit, thus enabling you to take back your life. I don't say 'take back your life' lightly, because we all know the health problems associated with smoking cigarettes and that is probably one of the main driving forces behind why you have decided to be smoke-free.

One thing we are not going to do during the Think Quit program is go on and on about all the related health issues. It is important, however, for you to be aware of the dangers of continuing to smoke so we will cover these issues briefly and you can use this section of the book to strengthen your resolve and give yourself more reasons to quit. You already know that smoking can cause stroke, cancer, heart attacks and clogging of the arteries. We won't waste time going into the finer details about gangrene or impotence, because you can read about these dangers on a packet of cigarettes.

We won't waste time *because you know all those health-related issues are actual fact*. If they weren't, why would health authorities and governments legislate that cigarette companies, by law, must print on their product such warnings as SMOKING CAUSES CANCER, SMOKING CAN HARM OTHERS, SMOKING CLOGS YOUR ARTERIES, and so on? Why would they have banned smoking on public transport and in many other public places, or while children are in the car? So we won't waste too much time talking about all the health issues because you already know that the moment you stop smoking you begin to regain your health, undoing harm and adding years to your life rather than cutting your life short.

Another major issue is obviously the financial one. For some people, this is not a problem, but for many it is. Calculate how much you spend a day, a week or a year on cigarettes. Some people spend three to four thousand dollars a year, some even more. Multiply that by ten years and it adds up to $30,000 to $40,000; multiply that by 20 years and you have spent $60,000 to $80,000. How much do you spend?

Recently, I was on the phone with a woman who had been a two-pack-a-day smoker for almost 50 years. At today's prices, this added up to approximately $400,000. That's almost half a million dollars. And her comment as she sobbed was 'For what?' She had lost count of the number of times she had attempted to stop smoking over the years. What really upset her was the fact that she had always struggled financially and never owned her own home. Now all she had to show for the years of smoking was ill-health.

I recently had a call from another woman who said that after using the Think Quit program it had been six months since her last cigarette, and she had just purchased a large-screen TV with the money she had saved. Every cent that would have been spent on cigarettes went into a piggy bank. Next on her wish list was an overseas holiday, something she could never have afforded while she was a smoker. I am sure there are many good things you could do with the money you save by not smoking.

Think Quit is about making a shift in your awareness and how you perceive smoking while forming new healthy habits and creating change in your unconscious mind—this is the key to your success.

Unfortunately, some people are frozen by the fear of failure: 'What if I tell everyone I'm quitting and I start smoking again? I'll be a failure.' Many people also worry that it will be too hard. They fear cravings, stress and nervous tension, losing control or gaining weight: 'I know someone who quit smoking and put on 10 kilos.' Maybe you even fear you will lose your best friend, your smoking buddy. Throughout Think Quit we will address all these challenges, all these issues, and you will have the tools to overcome each of them easily and effortlessly.

One of the main keys to success is to replace a bad habit with a good one. That is what much of this program is about: rewiring your thinking patterns, your physical behaviour and the way you relate to smoking. Once you replace the bad habits with good habits—and you will—quitting will be easy.

Being smoke-free can be easy, effortless and even enjoyable. The reality is that there is nothing at all in a cigarette that your body or your mind needs. Feel confident—every year there are one million people who become non-smokers.

Now it is your turn.

Tackle this challenge with a joyous attitude and get ready to celebrate.

As mentioned, we will be taking a twofold approach. You will be given the tools and skills to overcome any physical cravings.

You'll also be given the tools and support to change the way you think, to change the belief that you are a smoker, to change the emotional need or desire for a cigarette.

Think of yourself as a non-smoker from the moment you quit!

2 | *THINK QUIT*
PROGRAM METHODS

This chapter provides an overview of the therapies used throughout the Think Quit program. The main methods used are chi kung (pronounced chee-goong, and sometimes spelled qi gong), acupressure, neurolinguistic programming (NLP), hypnosis and some good old-fashioned motivation.

Chi kung

Chi kung originated in China approximately 7000 years ago and is the grandfather of both acupuncture and tai chi. The term chi kung literally translates as 'breathing exercise'. Chi means 'the life force' (i.e. the breath) and kung means 'the exercise'. We'll be using chi kung for several reasons: to reduce stress, to increase your body's healing ability and to help you breathe more deeply.

The simple exercises included in the book are designed to help you breathe more deeply and feel rejuvenated. Also, chi kung, with its natural, easy movements, is renowned for helping to reduce or remove stress. Many people say they are stressed and that smoking helps remove their stress, but this is a fallacy. The fact is, smoking causes dehydration in your body and this increases stress. Nicotine cravings increase stress. That is why when you have a cigarette you feel more relaxed—because you have just fulfilled the craving. But what is proven to truly reduce stress is deep breathing. You will never see a stressed-out tai chi master or yoga teacher. Chi kung is like a moving form of yoga; however, it includes breathing exercises that you do with minimal movement.

During a Think Quit seminar, I asked everybody in attendance whether they believed smoking reduced stress. There were around 80 long-term one- to two-pack-a-day smokers in the room and every single hand went up. It was unanimous: 'smoking reduces stress'. I then asked who currently felt they were stressed and the majority of hands went up. Next I requested that everybody join me at the windows, which overlooked a park. We then did a simple breathing exercise: we took a slow deep breath all the way in, held it for a moment, then exhaled slowly while silently saying the word 'relax' to ourselves. We repeated this ten times. When everyone was seated again, I asked who still felt stressed and not a single hand went up. This was the result of one simple breathing exercise that only took a few minutes. When I once again asked who believed smoking reduced stress, not a single hand went up.

Acupressure

Acupressure is like acupuncture without the needles. Laser therapy also uses acupuncture points when assisting people to stop smoking. In Think Quit, you will learn how to use a thumb or finger to apply pressure to a specific stop-smoking point as well as points that, when stimulated, will help strengthen your lungs and reduce feelings of fatigue or headache. Acupressure and acupuncture have been around for thousands of years and have stood the test of time. Today, many medical doctors utilise acupuncture to assist clients in their recovery from a wide range of health challenges. The acupressure points you will use are simple to learn and easy to remember.

Neurolinguistic programming

The third component is neurolinguistic programming (NLP), which is at the frontier of the study into how our mind works, how we motivate ourselves, how we achieve our goals, how we overcome fears and how we produce specific results. NLP also helps us understand and give meaning to our everyday experiences and behaviour. Through NLP, we have the tools to break free of old destructive patterns and habits while giving ourselves more choices.

NLP was created by Dr John Grinder and Dr Richard Bandler at the University of California, Santa Cruz, during the early seventies. Doctors Grinder and Bandler teamed up to study some of the most accomplished therapists in their chosen fields and researched the likes of Fritz Perls, the creator of gestalt therapy, Virginia Satir, the founder of family therapy, and Milton Erickson, the father of modern clinical hypnosis. By studying in detail the strategies of the experts and noting the lasting changes in their clients, the doctors were able to put together and create the therapeutic techniques that would bring about rapid and lasting change to anyone undergoing NLP.

NLP has also exposed us to the fact that everybody learns in a different way. Some people are more visual and learn by seeing. These people are likely to say things like: 'Show me what you mean', 'I get the picture', 'I clearly see', and so on. Others are more kinaesthetic, which means they learn from doing and operate more from a 'feeling' perspective. They might say, for example, 'That feels right', 'I have a handle on it' or 'I grasp what you are saying'. Then there are those who are more auditory: these people listen carefully to instructions and may say things like 'That rings true for me' or 'I hear you'.

Of course, we are all seeing, feeling, hearing creatures, so in everyday life we operate from all of these sensory modalities. However, one sense is usually more dominant than the others.

To establish your primary learning modality, read the following statements. As you do, note which one is most important to you.

A. I am ready to stop smoking mainly for my health and how good I will feel when I stop.
B. I have heard how dangerous smoking is and finally stopping smoking sounds like a great idea.
C. I would like to see myself as a non-smoker and I like the idea of a brighter, healthier, smoke-free future.

All three may appeal to you, but one will probably be more appealing than the others. If you preferred A, your learning style is kinaesthetic; if B, auditory; if C, visual.

NLP language patterns are used from time to time in the book to help you overcome your challenges. On Day 5 of your Seven-Day Preparation Program, we will use an NLP technique known as anchoring. Anchoring allows you to call on positive resources from your past to help you maintain an empowered state once you stop smoking.

Hypnosis

Another key method we will be using is hypnosis. Many people, when they hear the word 'hypnosis', think of somebody on a stage, maybe all in black, waving their hand around at people and making them do the chicken dance or sing like Elvis or talk on their shoe-phone, but this is simply for entertainment. Clinical hypnosis is not the same as stage hypnosis. With clinical hypnosis, suggestions are used to change your thinking in the unconscious part of your mind. These days hypnosis goes by many names, such as relaxation therapy, guided imagery and visualisation.

The *Journal of Applied Psychology* concluded in 1992 that hypnosis is the most effective way to stop smoking. Combining the results of more than 600 studies involving 72,000 people, the results showed hypnosis was three times more effective than nicotine replacement therapy and 15 times more effective than trying to quit alone. In 2005, the *Journal of Nursing Scholarship* published a study of 71 smokers. It reported that those using hypnosis were twice as likely to quit as those who quit on their own.

The most recent study was presented in October 2007 to the American College of Chest Physicians at their annual meeting. Of the 67 smokers involved in the study, 50 per cent of patients who used hypnosis were still smoke-free after six months compared with 25 per cent of patients who went cold turkey. Only 16 per cent of those using patches and gum remained smoke-free at the end of this period.

Think of yourself as a non-smoker from the moment you quit.

One benefit of hypnosis is that it induces a relaxed state in your body and allows your conscious mind to be distracted while your unconscious accepts suggestions such as: 'You are now smoke-free, you are now a non-smoker.' You take these suggestions on board and they become your way of thinking. Hypnosis accesses the imagination and allows us to experience thoughts and images as real.

It is widely accepted amongst hypnotherapists that all hypnosis is self-hypnosis. A hypnotist is not able to make you do something that would be in conflict with your core values or beliefs. Hypnosis is more of a 'do with' process than a 'do to' process.

All of the hypnosis sessions throughout this book are self-hypnosis. The fact is that you have already used a lot of negative self-hypnosis to make it difficult to stop smoking. This will be explained in more detail later. Think Quit, however, while dealing with a little bit of negative motivation, deals largely with positive suggestions such as 'I am now smoke-free', as well as positive visualisations (which are another form of self-hypnosis).

Self-hypnosis works by way of auto-suggestion. By feeding your mind positive suggestions, you will make stopping smoking so much easier. Your body and mind can be affected both positively and negatively depending on the thoughts and suggestions you are giving yourself. Tell yourself it will be difficult to stop smoking and it will be. On the other hand, when you train your unconscious mind to believe that it will be *easy* to stop, then this will also come true. Through repetitive positive affirmations, you are programming your mind in a way that supports you in reaching your goal of being smoke-free.

Mental visualisation helps to reinforce the self-hypnotic process, so throughout the book you will be asked to visualise specific outcomes such as seeing yourself as a non-smoker. In effect, you will be training your unconscious mind to think in a new and positive way, and your body to act in a way that will allow you to be smoke-free.

Milton Erickson, the father of modern-day clinical hypnosis, said: 'Hypnosis is a state of intensified attention and receptiveness to an idea, or a set of ideas.' Repetition will help to reinforce these ideas, and I'll be asking you to repeat several key phrases in your mind or out loud at each step of the way. The power of the mind is extraordinary, so let's harness that power to get the result you want. It is time to stop convincing yourself that stopping smoking will be difficult. It is time to stop convincing yourself that you will not survive the cravings. It is time to stop convincing yourself that you need cigarettes.

Here's a self-hypnotic suggestion that will help you change your thinking patterns:

> Stopping smoking is easy!
> Stopping smoking is easy!
> **Stopping smoking is easy!**

Repeat this phrase often in the lead-up to Q-Day. Even if at first you do not fully believe it, continue to repeat it over and over. In this way, you will convince yourself that it will be easy, and guess what? *It will be easy!* When you reach Q-Day, you could repeat it hundreds of times a day, like a mantra.

Think of yourself as a non-smoker from the moment you quit.

When you are able to let go of the decision you made to be a smoker and the belief you have that you are a smoker or you need cigarettes, then quitting is easy. You need to transform that belief into a new belief: *I am now a non-smoker.* Once you do this, quitting becomes easier.

You may have programmed yourself to believe quitting is hard and you won't be able to handle the cravings, that you won't know what to do with your hands, that you will lose your best friend, and so on. Henry Ford once said: 'If you think you can or think you can't, you are always right.' The fact is you *can* stop smoking and you *can* make it easier than you think. You will be able to handle the cravings. You will have plenty of things to do with your hands. And what sort of friend would inject you with 43 known carcinogenic (cancer-causing) chemicals?

Say to yourself right now: 'I CAN stop smoking and I WILL stop smoking!' Repeat this phrase three times quickly:

> I CAN stop smoking and I WILL stop smoking!
> I CAN stop smoking and I WILL stop smoking!
> I CAN stop smoking and I WILL stop smoking!

The key to stopping smoking lies in what you tell yourself and what your beliefs are. When you have re-evaluated and given new meaning to the old beliefs, all of a sudden the problem that seemed insurmountable disappears.

Changing your mindset by what you say to yourself, along with your replacement strategies, is really the crux of this program.

Think of yourself as a non-smoker from the moment you quit.

3 | COMMON METHODS USED TO GIVE UP SMOKING

While achieving some degree of success, most smoking-cessation methods, other than hypnosis, NLP or cognitive behavioural therapy, deal with only the physical aspect of stopping smoking. Almost all of the studies I have reviewed give different percentages of success for each method.

Cold turkey or willpower

The New Year is almost upon you. What is your top resolution for the coming year? To stop smoking and get healthy? So what happens? Maybe you party hard on New Year's Eve and at midnight you resolve to never touch another cigarette again. Does this sound familiar? Going cold turkey or using willpower alone can be a last-ditch attempt or a spur-of-the-moment thing. For some people, going cold turkey works; unfortunately, other people will struggle for a few hours and then they are smoking again. Without preparation and a plan, a high percentage of people who give up cold turkey fail. You need to tackle the desire to smoke and your reasons for doing so, otherwise at the first stressful event or your next social outing you will start smoking again. Different studies show a success rate of between 3 and 6 per cent.

Nicotine replacement therapies

Nicotine replacement therapies (NRT), such as nicotine patches, gum and inhalers, had variable success rates. The upside is that these therapies can help some people overcome physical cravings for nicotine. The downside with NRT is that they may not fully address the mental or emotional aspect of smoking.

I bumped into an old school friend recently who was chewing on gum. I was telling him about Think Quit and he said he had stopped smoking more than a year earlier and the gum he was chewing was nicotine gum. I was curious and asked how much he was spending on the gum each week. I was surprised by the fact that he was spending $50 per week, which worked out to be $2600 for the past year. (However, as a previously heavy smoker, he was only spending half the amount on gum than he had been spending on cigarettes.)

Zyban® (antidepressant)

Zyban® was initially used to help people with anxiety. Evidence has shown a success rate for quitting of around 15 per cent with the antidepressant pill. The downside is that there may be side-effects including insomnia, loss of appetite, agitation, nausea, constipation, numbness and headaches. Allergic reactions may include swelling of the lips, fainting and difficulty breathing.

Champix® (Varenicline)

Champix® is a prescription-only smoking-cessation medication taken in tablet form for a period of three months. It claims a one-in-five success rate. Champix® is reported to block the effects of nicotine on the brain and can also reduce cravings. About 30 per cent of people in clinical trials suffered nausea, and other side-effects have been reported. While the drug itself does not tackle the mental problems, the manufacturers have provided online information to help people battle the smoking triggers and provide additional motivation. The people in the trials did, however, receive 16 counselling sessions and were given a course of nicotine replacement therapy at the end of the 12-week trial.

Herbal stop-smoking products

There are a range of herbal stop-smoking products that may be beneficial, but it is difficult to find any studies or trials with significant results. Once again, these products do little to address the mental or emotional aspects of smoking.

Laser therapy

Laser therapy works by applying a low-intensity laser beam to specific points on the body. These points are the same as those used in acupuncture and acupressure. Laser therapy aims at increasing relaxation and reducing physical cravings. There have been no formal studies on the effectiveness of laser therapy, but some people I have spoken to have benefited from laser therapy and it goes some way towards helping with cravings and overcoming irritability.

4 | WHY DO YOU SMOKE?

People say they smoke for a variety of reasons: 'It relaxes me', 'I enjoy it', 'It makes me feel good.' But the main reason most smokers smoke is because they are addicted to nicotine and can't stop. Throughout this book, we will dispel the myths and remove the illusions. Beyond the cravings for the highly toxic drug nicotine (cravings that can easily be overcome) are the associations and triggers for smoking—which are all mental.

When did you start smoking?

I want you to consider why you started smoking in the first place. Was it peer pressure? Was it thinking you would look cool? Was it because you wanted to feel like a grown-up? Maybe you started smoking as a form of rebellion or to not feel 'left out' around others your age.

As a youngster, there is every likelihood that you took up smoking at least partly because you were influenced by direct or indirect advertising such as sponsorships of sporting or other events. This direct or indirect advertising portrayed smoking as a cool, exciting and invigorating thing to do.

Even the seemingly innocent candy cigarettes that so many people pretended to smoke as children have now been linked to people taking up smoking, and they have been banned in many countries, like Canada and the United Kingdom.

What about all the actors who smoked? In the past, actors seen to be the epitome of cool, from James Dean to John Wayne and Greta Garbo, all smoked, making it seem desirable and fashionable. It was too late for Yul Brynner when he realised the dangers of smoking. Brynner died in his sixties from lung cancer, and his famous last words were, 'Whatever you do … *don't smoke*.'

It is most likely that you were conditioned to smoking well before you had your first cigarette. If you are old enough to remember, think of Paul Hogan with the 'Anyhow' ads or the 'Marlboro Man' on his horse. Gomez Addams smoked in *The Addams Family*, as did Lucy and Desi Arnez in *I Love Lucy*. Good old Popeye smoked a pipe. Tom and Jerry smoked and there are numerous characters on *The Simpsons* who smoke. A study that appeared in the *New England Journal of Medicine* (24 March 1999) looked at 50 G-rated animated films made over the previous 60 years and found that more than two-thirds of animated children's films featured tobacco use in the story plots.

Did you ever smoke those candy cigarettes or candy cigars as a youngster? Did you ever take a pen or a pencil and pretend you were smoking?

One sinister campaign was the old Winston advertisement featuring characters from the animated TV series *The Flintstones*, with Barney advising Fred about how good Winston cigarettes are. If you would like to view the *Flintstones* Winston commercial, you can go to YouTube and type in 'Flintstones Winston'.

Mental addiction: triggers and associations

After years of smoking, you will have created powerful associations or triggers that connect smoking with other events. Some people associate smoking with almost everything they do.

Read through the following list and discover which triggers or smoking associations apply to you. Do you smoke:

- when you are stressed?
- when you feel bored?
- when you feel lonely?
- after a meal?
- when driving?
- while drinking coffee?
- while drinking alcohol?
- while watching TV?
- when socialising?
- when you are on the phone?
- as an escape?
- on a work break?
- immediately on waking up?
- before bed?
- at other times?

Write any other triggers in the space provided.

_____

_____

_____

_____

_____

_____

If you have smoked 20 cigarettes a day for 20 years, this adds up to a total of 146,000 cigarettes smoked. If you have ten triggers, such as the ones listed on page 34, then this adds up to almost 15,000 times each trigger or association has been reinforced.

When you say to yourself, 'A meal is not complete without a cigarette', then this becomes a habit and a belief. You have conditioned yourself to think and respond in certain ways. Think Quit will assist you in disconnecting all the current connections you have to smoking, including the belief that you are a smoker. Creating new conditioned responses is easier than you think. You will install new associations and new responses in your unconscious mind while being consciously aware of them.

Bear in mind that withdrawal symptoms from nicotine are temporary. With Think Quit, you will be a non-smoker before you know it. Nicotine, while an addictive substance, is nowhere near as hard to give up as you've probably been led to believe. Also, if you have attempted to stop using the cold turkey method with no real plan, no real change of mindset and no replacement strategies, then it might have been difficult. We've all heard the old saying, When you fail to plan, you plan to fail. As you give every exercise in this book a fair go and fill in your seven-day smoking diary, you will make stopping so much easier. You will have a plan. You will stick to that plan. And success will be yours.

5 | THE DANGERS OF SMOKING

I don't want to spend too much time dwelling on the well-known (and lesser-known) diseases caused by smoking, or go into all the sickening details of these illnesses, so I'm going to address them here and then move on to discuss the myriad health benefits of quitting. Some of the more common diseases caused by smoking do include oral cancer, throat cancer, oesophageal cancer, pneumonia, lung cancer, stomach cancer, bladder cancer, chronic cardiovascular and lung disease. But are you familiar with the new list of illnesses linked to smoking, such as leukaemia, pancreatic cancer, kidney cancer, cervical cancer, stomach cancer, abdominal aneurysm and hardening of the arteries? Then throw in the possibility of stroke, asthma, vision loss, discolouration of teeth, skin wrinkling and premature ageing, and you have many good reasons to quit. Here are some more well-known facts:

- Cigarette smoke contains more than 4000 chemicals—and more than 40 of those chemicals are carcinogenic (cancer-causing) toxic substances! Microscopic particles of these poisons enter your bloodstream via your lungs.
- Approximately half of all long-term smokers will die early from tobacco-related illness.
- In August 2006, *Science Daily*, based on the findings of University of Florida scientists, reported that cigarette smoke can turn

normal breast cells cancerous. The poisons found in the smoke block the ability of the cells to repair themselves, which can eventually lead to tumour development.

- Every cigarette smoked reduces your life by an average of five minutes.

According to the World Health Organization, smoking is the single largest preventable cause of disease and premature death in the world. Australia has 19,000 smoking-related deaths every year. Smoking is a prime factor in heart disease, stroke and chronic lung disease.

IT IS TIME TO STOP!

Here are some of the main poisons contained in cigarette smoke, and other places where they can be found:

- Ammonia—used in floor cleaner
- Arsenic—used in rat poison
- Butane—used for lighter fluid
- Cadmium—used in batteries
- Carbon monoxide—car exhaust fumes
- Formaldehyde—used to preserve body tissue in corpses
- Hydrogen cyanide—the poison used in gas chambers
- Methane—used in rocket fuel
- Nicotine—used in rat poison.

IT IS TIME TO STOP!

WHAT THEY DON'T WANT YOU TO KNOW

The list of 599 additives approved by the US Government for use in the manufacture of cigarettes was submitted by the five major American cigarette companies to the Department of Health and Human Services in April 1994. While these substances have been approved as food additives, they were not tested for burning, which changes their chemical properties.

Acetanisole Acetic Acid Acetoin Acetophenone 6-Acetoxydihydrotheaspirane 2-Acetyl-3-Ethylpyrazine 2-Acetyl-5-Methylfuran Acetylpyrazine 2-Acetylthiazole Aconitic Acid dl-Alanine Alfalfa Extract Allspice Extract,Oleoresin and Oil Allyl Hexanoate Allyl Ionone Almond Bitter Oil Ambergris Tincture Ammonia Ammonium Bicarbonate Ammonium Hydroxide Ammonium Phosphate Dibasic Ammonium Sulfide Amyl Alcohol Amyl Butyrate Amyl Formate Amyl Octanoate alpha-Amylcinnamaldehyde Amyris Oil trans-Anethole Angelica Root Extract, Oil and Seed Oil Anise Anise Star, Extract and Oils Anisyl Acetate Anisyl Alcohol Anisyl Formate Anisyl Phenylacetate Apple Juice Concentrate, Extract, and Skins Apricot Extract and Juice Concentrate 1-Arginine Asafetida Fluid Extract And Oil Ascorbic Acid 1-Asparagine Monohydrate 1-Aspartic Acid Balsam Peru and Oil Basil Oil Bay Leaf, Oil and Sweet Oil Beeswax White Beet Juice Concentrate Benzaldehyde Benzaldehyde Glyceryl Acetal Benzoic Acid, Benzoin Resin Benzophenone Benzyl Alcohol Benzyl Benzoate Benzyl Butyrate Benzyl Cinnamate Benzyl Propionate Benzyl Salicylate Bergamot Oil Bisabolene Black Currant Buds Absolute Borneol Bornyl Acetate Buchu Leaf Oil 1,3-Butanediol 2,3-Butanedione 1-Butanol 2-Butanone 4(2-Butenylidene)-3,5,5-Trimethyl-2-Cyclohexen-1-One Butter,Butter Esters, and Butter Oil Butyl Acetate Butyl Butyrate Butyl Butyryl Lactate Butyl Isovalerate Butyl Phenylacetate Butyl Undecylenate 3-Butylidenephthalide Butyric Acid] Cadinene Caffeine Calcium Carbonate Camphene Cananga Oil Capsicum Oleoresin Caramel Color Caraway Oil Carbon Dioxide Cardamom Oleoresin, Extract, Seed Oil, and Powder Carob Bean and Extract beta-Carotene Carrot Oil Carvacrol 4-Carvomenthenol 1-Carvone beta-Caryophyllene beta-Caryophyllene Oxide Cascarilla Oil and Bark Extract Cassia Bark Oil Cassie Absolute and Oil Castoreum Extract, Tincture and Absolute Cedar Leaf Oil Cedarwood Oil Terpenes and Virginiana Cedrol Celery Seed Extract, Solid, Oil, And Oleoresin Cellulose Fiber Chamomile Flower Oil And Extract Chicory Extract Chocolate Cinnamaldehyde Cinnamic Acid Cinnamon Leaf Oil, Bark Oil, and Extract Cinnamyl Acetate Cinnamyl Alcohol Cinnamyl Cinnamate Cinnamyl Isovalerate Cinnamyl Propionate Citral Citric Acid Citronella Oil dl-Citronellol Citronellyl Butyrate itronellyl Isobutyrate Civet Absolute Clary Oil Clover Tops, Red Solid Extract Cocoa Cocoa Shells, Extract, Distillate And Powder Coconut Oil Coffee Cognac White and Green Oil Copaiba Oil Coriander Extract and Oil Corn Oil Corn Silk Costus Root Oil Cubeb Oil Cuminaldehyde para-Cymene 1-CysteineDandelion Root Solid Extract Davana Oil 2-trans, 4-trans-Decadienal delta-Decalactone gamma-Decalactone Decanal Decanoic Acid 1-Decanol 2-Decenal Dehydromenthofurolactone Diethyl Malonate Diethyl Sebacate 2,3-Diethylpyrazine Dihydro Anethole 5,7-Dihydro-2-Methylthieno(3,4-D) Pyrimidine Dill Seed Oil and Extract meta-Dimethoxybenzene para-Dimethoxybenzene 2,6-Dimethoxyphenol Dimethyl Succinate 3,4-Dimethyl-1,2 Cyclopentanedione 3,5- Dimethyl-1,2-Cyclopentanedione 3,7-Dimethyl-1,3,6-Octatriene 4,5-Dimethyl-3-Hydroxy-2,5-Dihydrofuran-2-One 6,10-Dimethyl-5, 9-Undecadien-2-One 3,7-Dimethyl-6-Octenoic Acid 2,4 Dimethylacetophenone alpha,para-Dimethylbenzyl Alcohol alpha,alpha-Dimethylphenethyl Acetate alpha,alpha Dimethylphenethyl Butyrate 2,3-Dimethylpyrazine 2,5-Dimethylpyrazine 2,6-Dimethylpyrazine Dimethyltetrahydrobenzofuranone delta-Dodecalactone gamma-Dodecalactone para-Ethoxybenzaldehyde Ethyl 10-Undecenoate Ethyl 2-Methylbutyrate

Ethyl Acetate Ethyl Acetoacetate Ethyl Alcohol Ethyl Benzoate Ethyl Butyrate Ethyl Cinnamate Ethyl Decanoate Ethyl Fenchol Ethyl Furoate Ethyl Heptanoate Ethyl Hexanoate Ethyl Isovalerate Ethyl Lactate Ethyl Laurate Ethyl Levulinate Ethyl Maltol Ethyl Methyl Phenylglycidate Ethyl Myristate Ethyl Nonanoate Ethyl Octadecanoate Ethyl Octanoate Ethyl Oleate Ethyl Palmitate Ethyl Phenylacetate Ethyl Propionate Ethyl Salicylate Ethyl trans-2-Butenoate Ethyl Valerate Ethyl Vanillin 2-Ethyl (or Methyl)-(3,5 and 6)-Methoxypyrazine 2-Ethyl-1-Hexanol, 3-Ethyl -2 -Hydroxy-2-Cyclopenten-1-One 2-Ethyl-3, (5 or 6)-Dimethylpyrazine 5-Ethyl-3-Hydroxy-4-Methyl-2(5H)-Furanone 2-Ethyl-3-Methylpyrazine Ethylbenzaldehyde 4-Ethylguaiacol para-Ethylphenol 3-Ethylpyridine Eucalyptol Farnesol D-Fenchone Fennel Sweet Oil Fenugreek, Extract, Resin, and Absolute Fig Juice Concentrate Food Starch Modified Furfuryl Mercaptan 4-(2-Furyl)-3-Buten-2-One Galbanum Oil Genet Absolute Gentian Root Extract Geraniol Geranium Rose Oil Geranyl Acetate Geranyl Butyrate Geranyl Formate Geranyl Isovalerate Geranyl Phenylacetate Ginger Oil and Oleoresin 1-Glutamic Acid 1-Glutamine Glycerol Glycyrrhizin Ammoniated Grape Juice Concentrate Guaiac Wood Oil Guaiacol Guar Gum 2,4-Heptadienal gamma-Heptalactone Heptanoic Acid 2-Heptanone 3-Hepten-2-One 2-Hepten-4-One 4-Heptenal trans -2-Heptenal Heptyl Acetate omega-6-Hexadecenlactone gamma-Hexalactone Hexanal Hexanoic Acid 2-Hexen-1-Ol 3-Hexen-1-Ol cis-3-Hexen-1-Yl Acetate 2-Hexenal 3-Hexenoic Acid trans-2-Hexenoic Acid cis-3-Hexenyl Formate Hexyl 2-Methylbutyrate Hexyl Acetate Hexyl Alcohol Hexyl Phenylacetate 1-Histidine Honey Hops Oil Hydrolyzed Milk Solids Hydrolyzed Plant Proteins 5-Hydroxy-2,4-Decadienoic Acid delta- Lactone 4-Hydroxy-2,5-Dimethyl-3(2H)-Furanone 2-Hydroxy-3,5,5-Trimethyl-2-Cyclohexen-1-One 4-Hydroxy -3-Pentenoic Acid Lactone 2-Hydroxy-4-Methylbenzaldehyde 4-Hydroxybutanoic Acid Lactone Hydroxycitronellal 6-Hydroxydihydrotheaspirane 4-(para-Hydroxyphenyl)-2-Butanone Hyssop Oil Immortelle Absolute and Extract alpha-Ionone beta-Ionone alpha-Irone Isoamyl Acetate Isoamyl Benzoate Isoamyl Butyrate Isoamyl Cinnamate Isoamyl Formate, Isoamyl Hexanoate Isoamyl Isovalerate Isoamyl Octanoate Isoamyl Phenylacetate Isobornyl Acetate Isobutyl Acetate Isobutyl Alcohol Isobutyl Cinnamate Isobutyl Phenylacetate Isobutyl Salicylate 2-Isobutyl-3-Methoxypyrazine alpha-Isobutylphenethyl Alcohol Isobutyraldehyde Isobutyric Acid d,l-Isoleucine alpha-Isomethylionone 2-Isopropylphenol Isovaleric Acid Jasmine Absolute, Concrete and Oil Kola Nut Extract Labdanum Absolute and Oleoresin Lactic Acid Lauric Acid Lauric Aldehyde Lavandin Oil Lavender Oil Lemon Oil and Extract Lemongrass Oil 1-Leucine Levulinic Acid Licorice Root, Fluid, Extract and Powder Lime Oil Linalool Linalool Oxide Linalyl Acetate Linden Flowers Lovage Oil And Extract 1-Lysine] Mace Powder, Extract and Oil Magnesium Carbonate Malic Acid Malt and Malt Extract Maltodextrin Maltol Maltyl Isobutyrate Mandarin Oil Maple Syrup and Concentrate Mate Leaf, Absolute and Oil para-Mentha-8-Thiol-3-One Menthol Menthone Menthyl Acetate dl-Methionine Methoprene 2-Methoxy-4-Methylphenol 2-Methoxy-4-Vinylphenol para-Methoxybenzaldehyde 1-(para-Methoxyphenyl)-1-Penten-3-One 4-(para-Methoxyphenyl)-2-Butanone 1-(para-Methoxyphenyl)-2-Propanone Methoxypyrazine Methyl 2-Furoate Methyl 2-Octynoate Methyl 2-Pyrrolyl Ketone Methyl Anisate Methyl Anthranilate Methyl Benzoate Methyl Cinnamate Methyl DihydrojasmonateMethyl Ester of Rosin, Partially Hydrogenated Methyl Isovalerate Methyl Linoleate (48%) Methyl Linolenate (52%) Mixture Methyl Naphthyl Ketone Methyl Nicotinate Methyl Phenylacetate Methyl Salicylate Methyl Sulfide 3-Methyl-1-Cyclopentadecanone 4-Methyl-1-Phenyl-2-Pentanone 5-Methyl-2-Phenyl-2-Hexenal 5-Methyl-2-Thiophenecarboxaldehyde 6-Methyl-3,-5-Heptadien-2-One 2-Methyl-3-(para-Isopropylphenyl) Propionaldehyde 5-Methyl-3-Hexen-2-One 1-Methyl-3Methoxy-4-Isopropylbenzene 4-Methyl-3-Pentene-2-One 2-Methyl-4-Phenylbutyraldehyde 6-Methyl-5-Hepten-2-One 4-Methyl-5-Thiazoleethanol 4-Methyl-5-VinylthiazoleMethyl-alpha-Ionone Methyl-trans-2-Butenoic Acid 4-Methylacetophenone para-Methylanisole alpha-Methylbenzyl Acetate alpha-Methylbenzyl Alcohol 2-Methylbutyraldehyde 3-Methylbutyraldehyde 2-Methylbutyric Acid alpha-Methylcinnamaldehyde Methylcyclopentenolone 2-Methylheptanoic Acid 2-Methylhexanoic Acid 3-Methylpentanoic Acid 4-Methylpentanoic Acid 2-Methylpyrazine 5-Methylquinoxaline 2-Methyltetrahydrofuran-3-One (Methylthio)Methylpyrazine (Mixture Of Isomers) 3-Methylthiopropionaldehyde Methyl 3-Methylthiopropionate 2-Methylvaleric Acid Mimosa Absolute and Extract Molasses Extract and Tincture Mountain Maple Solid Extract Mullein Flowers Myristaldehyde Myristic Acid Myrrh Oil beta-Napthyl Ethyl Ether Nerol Neroli Bigarde Oil Nerolidol Nona-2-trans,6-cis-Dienal 2,6-Nonadien-1-Ol gamma-Nonalactone Nonanal Nonanoic Acid Nonanone trans-2-Nonen-1-Ol 2-Nonenal Nonyl

Acetate Nutmeg Powder and Oil Oak Chips Extract and Oil Oak Moss Absolute 9,12-Octadecadienoic Acid (48%) And 9,12,15-Octadecatrienoic Acid (52%) delta-Octalactone gamma-Octalactone Octanal Octanoic Acid 1-Octanol 2-Octanone 3-Octen-2-One 1-Octen-3-Ol 1-Octen-3-Yl Acetate 2-Octenal Octyl Isobutyrate Oleic Acid Olibanum Oil Opoponax Oil And Gum Orange Blossoms Water, Absolute, and Leaf Absolute Orange Oil and Extract Origanum Oil Orris Concrete Oil and Root Extract Palmarosa Oil Palmitic Acid Parsley Seed Oil Patchouli Oil omega-Pentadecalactone 2,3-Pentanedione 2-Pentanone 4-Pentenoic Acid 2-Pentylpyridine Pepper Oil, Black And White Peppermint Oil Peruvian (Bois De Rose) Oil Petitgrain Absolute, Mandarin Oil and Terpeneless Oil alpha-Phellandrene 2-Phenenthyl Acetate Phenenthyl Alcohol Phenethyl Butyrate Phenethyl Cinnamate Phenethyl Isobutyrate Phenethyl Isovalerate Phenethyl Phenylacetate Phenethyl Salicylate 1-Phenyl-1-Propanol 3-Phenyl-1-Propanol 2-Phenyl-2-Butenal 4-Phenyl-3-Buten-2-Ol 4-Phenyl-3-Buten-2-One Phenylacetaldehyde Phenylacetic Acid 1-Phenylalanine 3-Phenylpropionaldehyde 3-Phenylpropionic Acid 3-Phenylpropyl Acetate 3-Phenylpropyl Cinnamate 2-(3-Phenylpropyl)Tetrahydrofuran Phosphoric Acid Pimenta Leaf Oil Pine Needle Oil, Pine Oil, Scotch Pineapple Juice Concentrate alpha-Pinene, beta-Pinene D-Piperitone Piperonal Pipsissewa Leaf Extract Plum Juice Potassium Sorbate 1-Proline Propenylguaethol Propionic Acid Propyl Acetate Propyl para-Hydroxybenzoate Propylene Glycol 3-Propylidenephthalide Prune Juice and Concentrate Pyridine Pyroligneous Acid And Extract Pyrrole Pyruvic Acid Raisin Juice Concentrate Rhodinol Rose Absolute and Oil Rosemary Oil Rum Rum Ether Rye Extract Sage, Sage Oil, and Sage Oleoresin Salicylaldehyde Sandalwood Oil, Yellow Sclareolide Skatole Smoke Flavor Snakeroot Oil Sodium Acetate Sodium Benzoate Sodium Bicarbonate Sodium Carbonate Sodium Chloride Sodium Citrate Sodium Hydroxide Solanone Spearmint Oil Styrax Extract, Gum and Oil Sucrose Octaacetate Sugar Alcohols Sugars Tagetes Oil Tannic Acid Tartaric Acid Tea Leaf and Absolute alpha-Terpineol Terpinolene Terpinyl Acetate 5,6,7,8-Tetrahydroquinoxaline 1,5,5,9-Tetramethyl-13-Oxatricyclo(8.3.0.0(4,9))Tridecane 2,3,4,5, and 3,4,5,6-Tetramethylethyl-Cyclohexanone 2,3,5,6-Tetramethylpyrazine Thiamine Hydrochloride Thiazole 1-Threonine Thyme Oil, White and Red Thymol Tobacco Extracts Tochopherols (mixed) Tolu Balsam Gum and Extract Tolualdehydes para-Tolyl 3-Methylbutyrate para-Tolyl Acetaldehyde para-Tolyl Acetate para-Tolyl Isobutyrate para-Tolyl Phenylacetate Triacetin 2-Tridecanone 2-Tridecenal Triethyl Citrate 3,5,5-Trimethyl -1-Hexanol para,alpha,alpha-Trimethylbenzyl Alcohol 4-(2,6,6-Trimethylcyclohex-1-Enyl)But-2-En-4-One 2,6,6-Trimethylcyclohex-2-Ene-1,4-Dione 2,6,6-Trimethylcyclohexa-1,3-Dienyl Methan 4-(2,6,6-Trimethylcyclohexa-1,3-Dienyl)But-2-En-4-One 2,2,6-Trimethylcyclohexanone 2,3,5-Trimethylpyrazine 1-Tyrosine delta-Undercalactone gamma-Undecalactone Undecanal 2-Undecanone, 1 0-Undecenal Urea Valencene Valeraldehyde Valerian Root Extract, Oil and Powder Valeric Acid gamma-Valerolactone Valine Vanilla Extract And Oleoresin Vanillin Veratraldehyde Vetiver Oil Vinegar Violet Leaf Absolute Walnut Hull Extract Water Wheat Extract And Flour Wild Cherry Bark Extract Wine and Wine Sherry Xanthan Gum 3,4-Xylenol Yeast

When will you stop?

Most smokers think: 'I'll quit tomorrow.' Unfortunately, for many people tomorrow never comes, or if it does it is already too late. Studies show that smoking shortens the average person's life by seven to eight years. And smoking-related illnesses can be slow and painful killers:

- Emphysema slowly rots your lungs, leading to constant bronchitis and difficulty breathing.

- Lung cancer is caused by the tar and poisons found in tobacco smoke. Nine out of ten lung cancers are caused by smoking. Most people who get lung cancer die. Lung cancer is a very unpleasant way to die.
- Heart disease and strokes are much more common among smokers than non-smokers.

IT IS TIME TO STOP!

Here are some more negative effects of cigarettes:

- reduced sense of smell
- reduced sense of taste
- stained teeth
- plaque on teeth
- gum disease
- increased cavities
- ashtray breath
- dry lips
- ugly staining of fingers
- premature ageing and increased wrinkles
- anxiety about health problems caused by smoking
- stinging and itchy eyes
- blindness and cataracts
- cancer of the lips
- cancer of the mouth
- cancer of the throat
- cancer of the larynx
- cancer of the oesophagus
- liver cancer
- stomach cancer
- cancer of the pancreas

- colon cancer
- kidney cancer
- bladder cancer
- cancer of the cervix
- sore throat
- cough and increased phlegm
- shortness of breath
- decreased lung capacity
- reduced fitness
- increased susceptibility to colds and flu
- pneumonia
- asthma
- inflammation of the airways
- poor circulation
- chronic bronchitis
- emphysema
- blocked and weakened arteries of the heart
- raised blood pressure
- stomach ulcers
- increased risk of osteoporosis
- sperm deformity
- reduced number of sperm
- infertility in males
- impotence and erectile dysfunction
- increased period pains
- early menopause
- infertility in females
- leukaemia
- gangrene
- weakened immune system
- increased stress
- and finally, death.

Other than that, there's not much wrong with smoking except that children who are regularly exposed to cigarette smoke are more likely to get bronchitis and pneumonia in their first year of life. They are also at increased risk of suffering severe asthma attacks. Children whose parents smoke are more likely to become smokers.

Take charge of your health and your life now!

Remember you can reverse the dangers but not if you keep smoking.

IT'S TIME TO STOP!

FACE THE FACTS
The World Health Organization reported in 2004 that tobacco caused 5.4 million deaths. This is approximately one death every six seconds. The WHO also reported that tobacco was responsible for 100 million deaths during the twentieth century. It has estimated that by 2020 the death toll will be 10 million people every year.

My story

Some of my one-on-one clients have said to me: 'How would you know what it feels like? You don't smoke.' In fact, I did. I started smoking at a very early age—passive smoking, that is. Some of my earliest memories are of sitting with my grandmother as she chain-smoked. I developed severe asthma, and remember being admitted to hospital several times with terrifying asthma attacks and other breathing difficulties thinking I was going to die.

When I got older, did I continue to smoke when my grand-mother wasn't around? Yes, I did—on the train or the bus, on the way to school ... everywhere I went there were people smoking. At the doctor's surgery, people smoked while they waited to be seen, and even my doctor smoked; while I was seeing him for asthma, I was breathing in his second-hand smoke.

You'd think these early experiences would have made me so repulsed by cigarettes that I'd never take up smoking myself. But by the time I was in Year 9, I had succumbed to peer pressure, wanting to be seen as cool, wanting to be part of the in-group, so I started actively smoking at school. By the time I left school, I was a regular smoker. I tried to stop on a number of occasions but it never lasted more than a few hours or a day at the most. Like everybody, even though I had only smoked for a few years I was hooked. Thankfully one morning I woke up and couldn't breathe—remember, I was the kid with asthma. I felt like I was choking. I began coughing, and I kept coughing until a large lump of disgusting, gluggy black phlegm came out. It was almost the size of a golf ball. That was it. I screwed the cigarette packet up and threw it in the bin, and I never touched another cigarette. I had finally come to my senses.

My mother had a great saying: 'If you were meant to smoke you would have a chimney out of the top of your head.' The truth is, we do not have a chimney out of the top of our heads and the poisons simply accumulate as our bodies struggle to keep us healthy. It's time to take a stand and regain control.

Second-hand smoke

The smoke released from the end of a smouldering cigarette, known as sidestream smoke, and the smoke exhaled by a person smoking carry a range of health issues for the innocent bystander. It is one thing to poison yourself, but it is another thing altogether to knowingly inflict the poison on loved ones or strangers. The dangerous link between passive smoking and adverse effects on the health of those breathing the poisons has been well documented and is supported by almost every major medical and scientific body. Those working in smoky environments are at great risk; also, smoking in the presence of children is of great concern. The effects on children include increased respiratory problems such as coughing and wheezing, bronchitis, sudden infant death syndrome (SIDS), increased risk of asthma, and adverse effects on learning and awareness. Children of smoking parents are also more likely to take up smoking than children from non-smoking families. In adults, passive smoking can lead to heart attacks, lung cancer, strokes and many of the same health problems suffered by a smoker.

Third-hand smoke

Toxic particles and contamination from tobacco smoke remain long after a cigarette is extinguished. So even if somebody goes outside for a cigarette, the poisons are still present on their clothes and in their hair. Third-hand smoke is of concern to the health of small children and babies who may come into contact with the toxic particles. Dangerous particles in third-hand smoke include lead, arsenic, ammonia, cyanide and polonium, a highly radioactive carcinogen.

It almost makes you want to have your own HAZMAT (hazardous materials) team on standby after every cigarette—particularly before coming into contact with children.

It's time to stop smoking. It's your choice.

6 | THE HEALTH BENEFITS OF QUITTING

There are many reasons to stop smoking. The great news is that shortly you will be a non-smoker, and you will no longer have to worry about the massive adverse health effects of smoking. To inspire you, let's now have a look at some of the known benefits associated with stopping smoking.

- Within 20 minutes of stopping smoking, your blood pressure, pulse rate and body temperature return to normal.
- Within eight hours, the carbon monoxide level in your blood drops to normal. Smoker's breath begins to disappear (and you no longer smell like an ashtray).
- In as little as 24 hours, your lungs begin to work more efficiently and you breathe more easily as your body starts to heal itself.
- Within three days, your chance of having a heart attack decreases and your nerve-endings begin to redevelop.
- Within a few weeks, your circulation improves, your taste buds come alive and your sense of smell improves dramatically. Your chances of picking up an infection are decreased.
- Within two months, your circulation and lung function improve. Lungs become cleaner, there is reduced risk of infection, coughing is reduced, oxygen levels rise and fatigue is diminished. Within two weeks to three months, your lung function increases by up to 30 per cent.

- After one year, your chance of having a heart attack is reduced by half. The chance of getting cancer from smoking is also greatly reduced.
- After being smoke-free for five years, your cholesterol levels will be lower and your arteries less blocked, thereby reducing the risk of heart attack, stroke or cancer.
- After ten years, your risk of having a heart attack or stroke is similar to someone who has never smoked, and you will have added many years to your life.

Your positive motivation

I want you to think now about the real reasons you want to be *smoke-free*. Over the years, people have given me various reasons as to why they wanted to quit. Many people cite health concerns as the major reason, but also wanting to watch children or grandchildren grow up, not being held prisoner by nicotine, saving money instead of wasting it and not feeling like a social leper: 'I want to be around for my partner/grandfather/grandmother/father/mother/brother/sister/whoever' are all reasons that people give for wanting to stop.

But it is important to remember that you have to want to do this for yourself.

Ask yourself: 'What is the real reason I want to be smoke-free—what is the number one reason, the most important reason to stop smoking?'

Then ask yourself what other reasons you have for wanting to be smoke-free.

Really think about it—why do you want to quit? Why do you want to be a non-smoker?

In the space provided, write down all the reasons why you want to be a non-smoker. You may like to use coloured markers or pencils and make your reasons as bright and positive as you can. In the space underneath your reasons, you may even like to draw some pictures or symbols that represent your reasons and the benefits of being smoke-free.

Reasons to be smoke-free

_____

_____

_____

_____

_____

_____

7 | OTHER BENEFITS OF BEING SMOKE-FREE

As well as improved health, you will probably have other reasons for wanting to be smoke-free. Perhaps you resent the amount of money you spend on cigarettes, or the amount of time you've spent smoking over the years when you could have been pursuing healthier habits? Let's now have a closer look at these additional benefits to becoming a non-smoker.

Financial cost

Now take a few moments to work out the financial benefits of being a non-smoker. Write down how much you spend on cigarettes:

Daily $_____
Weekly $_____
Monthly $_____
Yearly $_____

Now rewrite your daily cost and then add four zeros:

Daily + 4 zeros = $_____

If you spend $10 per day over 27 and a half years, you will have spent approximately $100,000. If you spend $20 a day over

27 and a half years, you will have spent approximately $200,000 on cigarettes. That is a lot of money, even if you are well off.

So think about it: assuming you live to a reasonable old age, at $20 per day that's about half a million dollars. If there are two people in the family who smoke, that could add up to about one million dollars. I don't know about you, but I believe that rather than letting that money go up in smoke, there are a lot of things you could do with it throughout your life.

Here are some things people have bought with the money they've saved once they quit smoking:

- a new music system
- a new large-screen TV
- a new computer
- new DVDs and CDs
- new clothes
- new golf clubs
- a weekend away
- an overseas holiday
- a cruise
- a pushbike
- new hiking boots
- a trip in a hot-air balloon
- a helicopter ride
- personal training sessions
- regular massages
- a facial and other beauty therapies, such as a manicure or pedicure
- house renovations (or simply reducing the mortgage)
- new whitegoods
- a new wristwatch
- a new car

- dance classes
- a martial arts class
- a new hobby like pottery
- an art course or another field of study
- teeth whitening.

Now, write down a list of what you would like to spend the money on if you saved $100 a week, $400 per month or $5000 per year.

Let's now look at another crucial aspect of being smoke-free.

Time wasted

I appreciate that some smokers multi-task while having a cigarette, especially when at home, so the figures may vary depending on whether you are working from home and smoke inside or whether you are employed and need to leave the building to light up. However, quite a number of smokers I have spoken to over the years do not smoke inside the house.

The following example will help you estimate how much time is taken up in a single day by smoking.

Each time you have a cigarette, by the time you light up and smoke that cigarette and finish it, it equals five minutes (longer if you have to walk a fair way to have the cigarette). Five minutes is not much time on its own, but it adds up to a hundred minutes a day if you are smoking 20 cigarettes a day.

Total up your cigarettes, and write down how much time you spend smoking in a single day.

Number of cigarettes smoked daily = _____ ×
five minutes = _____

Go ahead now and add four zeros on to the end of that number. When you add the four zeros, that's roughly how much time you will spend smoking in the next 27 and a half years. If you smoke 20 cigarettes a day it equals one million minutes. This is the equivalent of around 16,500 hours or almost 700 days. It is almost two years—and that's if you smoke only one 20-cigarette pack a day. If you are a two-pack-a-day smoker, it would be four or five years.

Work it out yourself: based on a 20-cigarette packet, if you were to smoke one packet a day for the majority of your life, it would end up being approximately four to five years of wasted time. And as well as the wasted time, you have the increased danger of ill-health and cutting short your life by at least seven years.

Once you become smoke-free, you will not only have increased health but you are looking at years of a better-quality life. Many people say you have to die of something, and that's true—but why end up dying of emphysema, mouth cancer, lung cancer, gangrene or any of the other illnesses caused by smoking cigarettes? You wouldn't go and wrap your lips around the exhaust pipe of a car and get someone to start up the motor while you sucked on the fumes, would you?

Just one of the many toxic substances in cigarette smoke is methane gas, and you probably know that one of the greatest sources of methane is cow farts. Once again, if you were driving through the countryside and saw a cow, would you pull up, jump the fence, run over to the cow, wrap your mouth around the cow's butt and say 'Let one rip'?

8 | HOW TO COPE WITH NICOTINE WITHDRAWAL

Many people keep putting off the decision to quit smoking because they're worried about experiencing nicotine withdrawal symptoms. Here I'll address what people may experience, as well as suggesting some solutions to any temporary discomfort you might face.

It helps to bear in mind that any unpleasant side-effects of withdrawal are only temporary. Stopping smoking does not have to be hard work. As you carefully read every word on every page of this book, you will learn numerous replacement strategies and exercises that will help you to overcome the desire to smoke.

The majority of Think Quit clients actually claim they went through very few, if any, cravings. Why? When you reprogram your mind to think a different way, any cravings you might experience really have no power over you. When you follow the steps in Think Quit, you greatly reduce or eliminate the side-effects of stopping.

Some persistence is required, but then you already know you're a persistent person, don't you? You have persisted in smoking all these years. Think back to that first cigarette. Remember how your body rejected it. Maybe you felt dizzy and coughed, maybe you turned a light shade of green and felt ill. But you persisted, didn't you? You forced yourself to have another and another, until your brain and body made the necessary adjustments to be able to cope with the poison.

Your mind and body need somewhere between one and four weeks to adjust back to normal after years of drug addiction.

Possible withdrawal symptoms

The following symptom list includes most of the symptoms people may experience when they stop smoking using the usual methods. Keep in mind that most people only ever suffer from a few of these symptoms, never all of them. Even if you experience some of these symptoms, they won't last for long.

More of these symptoms occur when you simply go cold turkey and are not prepared. By using Think Quit, you are arming yourself with coping strategies and there is a greatly reduced chance of suffering from these smoking withdrawal symptoms:

- anxiety
- constipation
- cough
- craving for a cigarette
- dry mouth
- fatigue
- feelings of loss
- headache
- irritation, crankiness or anger

- insomnia
- inability to concentrate
- mild depression
- runny nose
- sore throat
- sore tongue and/or gums
- tightness in the chest
- 'quitter's flu'.

To reduce the chance of being affected by some of these symptoms, it may be a good idea to start taking some additional vitamins sooner rather than later. Talk to your doctor, pharmacist or health shop professional and find out the best vitamins to take for what you are undertaking. At the same time, start drinking more water and eating more nutritious meals. We'll discuss the importance of nutrition in the next chapter.

Solutions to this list of possible symptoms can be found on pages 219–23.

9 | BUT IF I STOP SMOKING, WILL I PUT ON WEIGHT?

Unfortunately many people put off quitting because they're concerned that they'll pile on the kilos once they stop smoking. But you will only put on weight if you replace the smoking habit by eating refined starchy carbohydrates and sugar-rich foods. You may also put on weight if you do not include some type of physical activity in your day. If you were a 20-cigarette-a-day smoker and you start to eat 20 biscuits a day, or a packet of sweets, then you are bound to put on weight.

You will not put on weight when you follow all the replacement strategies found in Think Quit! If you do put on a kilo or two, you will now be able to use all the time wasted on smoking to incorporate some fat-burning activity in your day. With the money you save, you could easily afford a personal trainer once a week or pay for a gym membership! With the extra energy you have and your increased lung capacity, you will feel fantastic.

The key to not putting on weight is eating healthy, balanced meals and increasing your activity.

All these healthy choices—and that is what they are, YOUR CHOICES—will help you to become healthier and more energetic and feel more alive. What's more, they will greatly reduce the risk of contracting the serious illnesses listed earlier in this book. We'll discuss diet in more detail in Part II.

10 | A 100 PER CENT COMMITMENT

The most crucial aspect of the Think Quit program is you. You have to make the choice, the conscious decision to be smoke-free. When you make a 100 per cent commitment to succeed and become smoke-free, you will find it easy. If you are half-hearted or not 100 per cent committed, you will likely end up failing. Instead of talking yourself down, talk yourself up.

Tomorrow will be Day 1 of your Seven-Day Preparation Plan. The following steps will be a major contributing factor to your ability to be smoke-free and to ensure your success. The more prepared you are, the easier it will be to stop smoking. Following each step of the program means you are serious about stopping smoking and you are ready to be smoke-free forever.

It is very important that you follow this program step by step. Start at the beginning and work your way through, following the suggestions and taking on board the ideas that will help you to become a non-smoker, and be smoke-free for the rest of your life.

Before commencing your Seven-Day Preparation Plan, it is important to understand why you want to stop. The previous chapters have given you plenty of reasons for quitting, and have dispelled many of the myths you may have heard, as well as the fears and anxieties you may feel about taking this positive step to improve your health and rid yourself of cigarettes once and for all. But more important than any reasons I have given you are your own personal reasons for becoming a non-smoker. Once you answer the following questions, you will be ready to start the Seven-Day Program. Writing down the answers to the questions and then reading over them is much more powerful than a momentary thought. This exercise will help you to better understand why you smoke and why you want to stop.

What kind of smoker are you?

It is important for you to know whether smoking is just something you do out of habit—for example, at special social occasions—or whether it is how you identify yourself. This is a very important question. I'd like you to stop reading and write the answer now. What does smoking mean to you—really think about it—and why do you smoke?

_____

_____

Next, ask yourself whether you identify as a smoker. If the answer is yes, then smoking has become so ingrained that it has become an important part of your life.

Why did you start smoking?

Now I want you to write down why you started smoking in the first place. Remember that first cigarette. Think back to when you actually became a regular nicotine addict.

What are the reasons you started?

_____

_____

Did you start smoking to be 'grown up', to be 'cool', to be an 'adult'? If you did, it is time to realise there are plenty of ways to be really 'cool' without touching a cigarette. If you started smoking to look older, it seems to have worked, doesn't it? It has been proven that smoking ages you prematurely and shortens your life. The majority of people now look upon smoking as a disgusting habit and ask about smokers: 'How can they inhale cigarette smoke into their lungs knowing it can kill them?'

Some smokers I talk to even say: 'When I look at other smokers I am disgusted, but I just can't seem to stop.'

This may or may not be what you are beginning to think to yourself. You may be starting to ask: 'How can I continue to poison myself? How can I continually put this smoke and all the thousands of chemicals into my body?' Knowing what you know, it seems crazy doesn't it? It is crazy!

Reasons for continuing to smoke

What are your reasons for smoking now? Again, really think about it. Could it be to relieve stress or to make you calm?

In light of what you know now and your decision to stop smoking, what are your reasons for continuing to smoke?

_____

_____

Didn't really need much time on that list, did you!

If you wrote down as one of your reasons 'to deal with stress' or 'to relax', I'd like you to quickly cross it out now, as that is an illusion and you need to let go of that thought. The fact is that smoking increases stress by constantly bombarding your body with poisons and dehydrating you.

Health

Now write down all the health benefits of smoking, of continuing to be a smoker.

_____

_____

The previous space should be completely blank. There are no health benefits of smoking. If you wrote anything in the space provided, quickly cross it out now. Remember, there is nothing in a cigarette your body needs.

Repeat three times:

There is nothing in a cigarette my body needs.
There is nothing in a cigarette my body needs.
There is nothing in a cigarette my body needs.

Reasons for becoming smoke-free

For years, you may have consciously rationalised why it was OK to smoke. Over this time, your mind became totally desensitised to the fact that you were slowly poisoning yourself.

The time has come to think about all the reasons you want to be smoke-free.

What are the three most important reasons why you want to be smoke-free? Really think about it. Why do you want to quit? Why do you want to be a non-smoker?

Now write down your top three reasons for wanting to be a non-smoker for the rest of your life.

Benefits of being smoke-free:

1 _____

2 _____

3 _____

Next, I'd like you to write down all the other reasons why you want to be smoke-free.

Additional reasons to be smoke-free:

_____

_____

_____

_____

_____

_____

What is important to you about not smoking?

Make a list of what's important to you. I could give you a list containing a thousand benefits, but this is about what YOU believe is most important to you in your life.

I'll start you off with a few ideas: *I'll stop smelling like an ashtray, I'm going to be able to smell the true aroma of foods, I'll be able to smell the sweet perfume of flowers with greater sensitivity, I'll have more energy, I won't cough as much, I'll look better, I'll be turning back the hands of time and improving my health, I'll be saving money.*

Write down all the benefits you can think of—these could be social benefits, such as no longer affecting your family or friends with cigarette smoke; it could simply be feeling good about not having to hide to have a smoke. I want you to take a few deep breaths and really think about the benefits. Take your time and when you get to the end of the list and think, 'This is as many benefits as I can think of,' keep going: you may come up with even more benefits of being a non-smoker.

_____

_____

_____

_____

_____

_____

_____

_____

_____

_____

Your reward list

Write down a list of all the things you would like to buy for yourself with the money saved by being smoke-free. The gifts could be for you or your family. You could break the list down into 52 weekly gifts, 12 monthly gifts, four quarterly gifts or one big present at the end of the year.

_____

_____

_____

_____

_____

_____

_____

_____

_____

Now that you've put all your reasons down on paper, and come up with a plan as to how you will spend the saved money, you should be thoroughly motivated to quit smoking for good.

Over the next seven days, you will undertake a doable step-by-step program enabling you to quit successfully. Enjoy the process as you discover how to overcome the old habit and become smoke-free forever.

PART II | The Seven-Day Preparation Program

'THIS TOO SHALL PASS'

King Solomon was troubled by thoughts that his feelings of satisfaction were only temporary and would not last, and that his feelings of sorrow would go on forever. He felt he could not see his way forward. He realised what he thought was satisfying him was only superficial. He asked his advisers to find him a ring he had seen in a dream. He believed this ring would ease his suffering. Eventually one of his advisers had a jeweller make a simple gold ring for the king. The words 'This too shall pass' were inscribed on the ring. When he read these words, the king's sorrows turned to joy. These four simple words, 'This too shall pass', gave him the true wealth and happiness for which he was searching.

BEFORE YOU
GET STARTED

On the following pages, you will find exercises designed for a specific outcome: to help you become and stay smoke-free. Some parts of this program may seem a little unusual to you, but I promise that if you follow all the steps they will add up to a positive result and your success.

During the next seven days, you may continue to smoke. You do not have to cut down, although some people do. That is entirely up to you.

You will find short affirmations at the beginning of each day's reading. Repeat these affirmations over and over. Make them your mantra for the day. As you do this, you will be reinforcing the positive messages to yourself.

If you have made several previous attempts to quit, don't despair. Maybe the methods you used were just not suitable for you. Maybe the time was not right. Maybe you did not have the right motivation. But now is the right time and the methods you will be using will make stopping far easier than it has been in the past, and much easier than you may have imagined.

If you stop smoking right now, you will not spend days or weeks suffering and rolling around in pain like a heroin addict would. This must tell you that the desire to quit is within your reach. Not only that, but nicotine is more poisonous than cocaine, heroin, ice (methamphetamine) and other highly poisonous drugs. These can kill you faster than cigarettes only because the level of toxicity in one drug hit is more concentrated than a cigarette hit. The amount of nicotine that you are slowly consuming in your cigarettes would kill you just as quickly if you had it in one hit. There's no doubt that smoking does kill—it just takes longer because you are taking your poison in minute amounts. Cigarettes are one of the leading causes of preventable death in Australia and the world: tobacco was responsible for approximately 90 per cent of drug-caused deaths in the 2004–05 period, and smoking caused 14 times as many deaths as alcohol in the same period.

Your contract with yourself

On the following page is a contract (agreement) you need to read carefully and sign. It is a contract with yourself. Too often, people take a half-hearted approach to their decision to stop smoking. By filling in and signing this contract, you are agreeing to hold yourself responsible for your actions and achieving your goal of becoming smoke-free forever. You need to work out when your Q-Day will be, bearing in mind that you will need a few days to read Part I of the book and seven days to work your way through the Seven-Day Preparation Program.

AN AGREEMENT made this _____ day of _____ in the year _____
Between _____ (referred to as 'the old me')
And _____ (referred to as 'the new me')

My Q-Day is the _____ day of _____ in the year _____

1. Commitment to being smoke-free
   (a) From the Q-Day date set out above, the new me refuses to put cigarette smoke in my body.
   (b) The new me will make healthy food choices that are in line with my goals.
   (c) The new me pledges and agrees to make all efforts to be active at least once per day.
   (d) The new me undertakes to live a more colourful, fulfilling and healthy life.
   (e) The new me will drink between 1 and 2 litres (six to eight glasses) of water every day.
   (f) The new me will avoid situations where I may be tempted to smoke.
   (g) If third parties, including without limitation other individuals, attempt to tempt me with cigarettes the new me will politely say 'No, thank you'.
   (h) The old me will not act in any way so as to affect the efforts of the new me in becoming smoke-free and remaining that way.
2. In the event that this agreement is breached in any way, the new me will commit to immediately re-focusing on the reasons for wanting to be smoke-free, stop smoking and stick to the plan.
   (a) Clause (2) is not to be used in any way to avoid the obligations of Clause 1. Clause (2) is only to be used as a safety mechanism to get back on track in the unlikely event of briefly losing sight of one's goal.

AGREED AND SIGNED by the old me: AGREED AND SIGNED by the new me:

_____   _____

Date: _____   Date: _____

Witness: _____   Witness: _____

(If no witnesses are available, you may also sign in the witness space, but bear in mind that you will be held even more responsible for your own actions.)

How you will succeed with *Think Quit*

For the next seven days, you will learn how to control stress. You will learn how to replace the cravings and how to gain control over your habits. You will learn how to let go of any *limiting beliefs* you may have. As mentioned, you don't have to cut back on smoking during the next seven days unless you choose to do so, but you will need to fill in your daily smoking diary (discussed further below). During this time, you will be preparing to become smoke-free forever. When you arrive at Q-Day, a little over a week from now, you will repeat to yourself: *I am now ready. Today is the day to be smoke-free. I am now a non-smoker.*

Before you start, think about a way to celebrate your Q-Day. You may like to book yourself in for a massage or facial. You could plan to plant a vegetable garden or flowerbed (if you live in a unit, you could get a planter box). You may decide to take a relaxing train trip to the country, go bushwalking and breathe the fresh air, or you may decide to visit some gardens or walk through a park. You could plan to spend a day at the beach and go fishing, or you could join a meditation class. Perhaps plan to visit non-smoking friends or relatives or clean out the garage or all your drawers or cupboards. You might like to spend a few days at a health retreat. Visit www.innermakeover.com.au for details on specific stop-smoking weekends and week-long retreats. On the other hand, you may decide to stay home and listen to the radio or watch some DVDs and do nothing. You may decide to tell everybody you are stopping or you may choose to tell nobody and just surprise them. Whatever feels right to you is best! How you spend your Q-Day is up to you. This is an important turning point in your life. You will finally be free.

It is important that you follow all the steps of the Think Quit program. If you decide to cut out any steps, you will be reducing your chance of becoming a non-smoker. All the steps are there for a reason: to help and support you in becoming smoke-free. It is up to you to diligently and enthusiastically follow each and every task and every exercise so you can be smoke-free before you know it—easily. As you go through each exercise in this book, decide what works best for you, which exercises you feel benefit you most. Take those exercises and own them—make them your own. If you enjoy the breathing exercises, you might decide to take up a yoga or tai chi class, or buy a book or DVD on yoga breathing.

There are a number of measures and steps you need to take to guarantee success. The first thing you need to do is make sure you are eating healthily—this is absolutely crucial. The second is to make sure you are drinking between 1 and 2 litres of water every day.

The other simple thing you will do on Day 1 is some deep-breathing exercises—nothing too fancy or complicated.

More about hydration

When you are smoking, your body dehydrates and your cells begin to dry up and shrink. You only have to look at someone who has been smoking for 30, 40 or 50 years and you will see that smoking increases ageing by dehydrating the skin over the entire body. It is essential to your goal of quitting and for better health that you start to hydrate your body over the next seven days in preparation for becoming smoke-free by drinking 1 to 2 litres of water a day.

The fact is, you lose water simply by breathing, and you can see proof of this when you breathe out on to glass—it's the water content in your breath that makes the glass fog up. You also perspire and go to the bathroom—together, this all adds up to between 2 and 2.5 litres of water a day. This lost fluid needs to be replaced so you will remain hydrated.

Be aware of the sugar content in drinks as well as in food—sugar in your blood turns to fat if it isn't burnt up by activity, so always check labels for sugar content. It is advisable not to drink so-called energy drinks, which are high in sugar, caffeine or artificial sweeteners and cause an increased heart rate, mood swings, dizziness and dehydration. Instead, sip on soda water or still or sparkling mineral water, or drink green tea or herbal teas. A fresh vegetable or no-added-sugar fruit juice like those found at many juice bars is great for your health.

More about diet

It is important that over the next seven days you seriously examine what you eat, and that you continue to eat healthily over the following weeks. So what is a healthy meal plan? You need to eat for nutrition. Choose a balance of healthy foods including protein, vegetables, fruit and grains. About every three to four hours during the day, to maintain balanced sugar levels have a small amount of nutritious food, such as carrot and celery sticks, a few spoonfuls of yoghurt or a piece of fruit. Each morning, make sure you eat a healthy breakfast such as porridge, eggs on toast or a protein shake. If you skip breakfast, your metabolism will slow down and this will lead to fat retention.

Make sure meals consist of mostly low GI foods, as these have a slower rate of digestion, making you feel less hungry for longer. The Glycaemic Index is a measure of how carbohydrates affect your blood sugar levels. Low GI foods include the majority of fruits and vegetables, multigrain breads, porridge or natural muesli, brown rice, wholemeal pasta, legumes and pulses such as beans and lentils, low-fat milk and proteins such as fish, eggs, lean meats and white low-fat cheeses. Incorporating low GI foods into your daily eating plan will help you cope with any sugar cravings.

High GI foods should be avoided. These include starchy breakfast cereals like corn flakes and rice bubbles, watermelon, white bread and pastries. In general, cut back on all starchy refined carbohydrates, such as cakes, biscuits, lollies and deep-fried foods. Any foods high in sugar or wheat flour often cause an insulin surge, and this leads to increased hunger.

As discussed in Part I, some people worry that if they stop smoking they will put on weight. The explanation for this is that for some people the cravings that are no longer being satisfied with a cigarette become cravings for more sugar. This is simply because you are not eating a balanced diet and keeping your sugar levels balanced. If you are still worried about your weight, check the back of this book for weight-loss resources.

Cravings

I want you to think again about addiction and what it means. Some people may experience strong cravings when they quit smoking, but there are also many people who never suffer a single craving, or only a few cravings here and there. If you do suffer, you can easily overcome the cravings with the tools and steps outlined here in your Seven-Day Preparation Program.

A craving only lasts up to three minutes; as each day passes, any urges to smoke will ease. By the ninth or tenth day, those cravings will be gone.

When you have the tools and strategies to nip any craving in the bud, the whole process becomes easier and you will feel so good knowing that the nicotine and the thousands of accumulated toxins in your body are leaving your system. It will be great to know that, as you breathe deeply, you are oxygenating your body with fresh air and adding years to your life.

Stress management

Over the next seven days, you will be arming yourself with stress-management tools and relaxation techniques that will give you a release valve for stress. It is no good to put a cap on the stress and try to deal with it that way—you want to learn how to let it go, how to transform the stress and release the build-up.

Now bear in mind as you practise the exercises described later that you will be learning how to let go of tension. Many people claim that the main reason they started smoking again after quitting for maybe three days, ten days, a month, three months or even six months was that they experienced stress or a traumatic event. So think about it for a moment. If you knew you had one of the most powerful relaxation and de-stressing tools at your disposal, if you could let go of tension and stress quite easily and effortlessly, would there be any need to ever consider a cigarette again?

Learning to relax can be done in a number of ways. You can learn yoga, meditation or tai chi. Simply lying in a bath with some relaxing music playing is a great way to unwind. The easiest and fastest way to relax, however, is so simple that you will surprise yourself at how quickly you can do it.

Are you ready? Slow your breathing down and count each breath backwards from ten until you reach zero. As you count each number, instruct yourself to double your relaxation with every breath. As you exhale, repeat one word in your mind. Your word could be *soften, relax, calm, peace, harmony, tranquillity*, or any other word that will help you to relax. This relaxation technique will only take a few minutes, yet it will leave you feeling calm and relaxed. If you like, you could repeat the process several times in a row for a deeper state of relaxation. You could enhance the process by lighting a candle in a quiet room and playing some soothing music. You could even turn this into a meditation and repeatedly count back from ten to zero for a period of 15 to 20 minutes.

Physical activity to combat agitation

If you feel agitated or nervous, you can burn it up with activity. Aim to be active every day and you will go a long way towards preventing feelings of agitation or nervous energy. Here are some ways to burn up and turn off that agitation:

- Go for a power walk or jog.
- Hit a tennis ball against a wall.
- Play hand ball.
- Swim.
- Stretch.
- Shadow box.
- Hit a punching bag.
- Join a fitness class.
- Join a martial arts class.

Enlisting a quit buddy

Once you have set the date of your Q-Day, contact several supportive friends or family members and tell them when you are planning to quit and that you would appreciate their support. You may like to even come up with a job description for your quit buddy (or buddies). When interviewing possible applicants, check that they will be supportive, encouraging, understanding and positive. You may ask them to either call you or check that they are happy for you to call them should the need arise. Your support person should have a copy of your replacement strategies, along with a list of your main reasons as to why you want to be smoke-free. They can then use this list to your advantage should you need the help.

Seven-day smoking diary

One of the most important things you will be doing over the next seven days is keeping a smoking diary, which you'll find at the back of the book. As mentioned, you don't have to cut back on smoking during the next seven days, unless you choose to do so. However, it is important that you diligently record every cigarette you have and follow the simple exercises.

In the space provided at the back of the book, you will note down every time you have a cigarette, no matter how few or how many you have each day. It is very important that you write down *every* cigarette.

You also have to write down exactly what triggered the craving or urge to smoke. Maybe you had a coffee or someone said, 'Let's have a cigarette.' Perhaps you saw something that made you want a cigarette. Whatever caused the need in you—the trigger—write it down. Then note down how the cigarette made you feel while you smoked it, and how you felt after you finished the cigarette. Keep it short. You could write something as brief as: 'Tea break. Felt calm. Felt relieved.' It could be 'Break with Tom.' It could even be 'Why am I doing this?' or 'I felt guilty.'

You must fill in the diary for every single cigarette you smoke throughout the day. Even if some of your reasons are the same each time, it is absolutely crucial that you make your entry in the diary after every single cigarette. This is a small price to pay, to write for 30 or 60 seconds, even up to 15 or 20 times a day, compared with the price you will pay if you don't become smoke-free. I cannot emphasise enough how essential this step is for your success in becoming smoke-free and staying that way for the rest of your life.

Don't rely on your memory or try to catch up later—it won't work. If you can't carry the diary at all times, then carry a pen and paper for notes and transfer your comments into the diary later.

I have found that face-to-face clients who filled in their diaries accurately and without omission have been successful and remain smoke-free. Some of my first clients, who were very keen to be smoke-free but not keen to make daily entries in their diaries, still wanted to go on with the sessions, and I obliged because of their pleas and apparent need to stop smoking (often for health reasons). Some of these clients did not achieve the same success as those who filled in their diaries. So these days I will not continue working with a client unless they show that their diary is completely filled in, as instructed.

There is a very important reason for the diary entries. At the end of the week, when you add up how many times you smoked when you were stressed or because you were influenced by others, how many times you smoked because you were on a break, and how many times you smoked because you were angry and so on, the results are assessed to provide vital information that will help you overcome your own specific challenges. By writing in your smoking diary every day, you are going to know exactly why you smoke. You could think about it, or simply tell a friend your thoughts and feelings, but that is not enough. You need to record it, you need to see it. Writing it down is part of the healing process.

You must also write down whether at the same time you are having an alcoholic drink, a coffee, a Coke, even a particular thought—it is all important.

Have a quick look at the back of the book now and you will see the seven-day smoking diary as well as a sample page so you have a good idea on how to fill it in.

Daily sessions

Each day there will be a different self-hypnosis session to read through. There will also be daily exercises to practise, from breathing and chi kung exercises to filling in your smoking diary.

Self-hypnosis

Self-hypnosis sessions are specific visualisation scripts that include positive suggestions. You can either read through the self-hypnosis sessions yourself or you could have a friend or family member read them to you. Alternatively, check the resources at the back of the book, as all the hypnosis sessions along with a number of additional sessions have been digitally recorded.

Deep-breathing and meditation exercises

During the course of the Seven-Day Preparation Program, you will learn some very simple deep-breathing exercises that will allow you to control and crush any cravings you might experience. You can practise these breathing exercises in a park, sitting down at work, lying down in bed, walking along—in fact, almost anywhere.

As discussed, the majority of people who relapse cite stress or a traumatic event as the major reason why they began smoking again. As you arm yourself with the tools and strategies to cope with the stress in your life, you will be another step closer to being a non-smoker—to being smoke-free for the rest of your life. One of the key ways we will do this in the Think Quit program is by deep-breathing and meditation exercises, such as the three exercises that follow. The more deeply you breathe, the more chi you circulate throughout your body. Chi is the life-force/energy-flow that runs through all living things. The more chi you have flowing through you, the more vitality you have. Eventually this relaxation will become second nature to you—imagine being able to just let go and relax at will. You will have the strategy to overcome stressful situations at any time.

The following relaxation exercises are calming techniques that will allow you to enter a deep state of relaxation in a relatively short period of time. After they stop smoking, some people have difficulty sleeping or feel anxious for a period of time, so this is a great exercise to help you unwind and get off to sleep (or back to sleep should you wake in the middle of the night). These exercises are great for helping you to feel calm and relaxed. They will also help you to familiarise yourself with relaxation. You can use these exercises at any time to de-stress. You could even combine the three exercises together simply moving from one to the next.

If you haven't done meditation or relaxation exercises before, read through the following instructions a few times until you understand how to do this meditation; you will find it is very easy and natural to do. Three dots indicate a short pause. The first exercise takes between four and five minutes, depending on the speed at which you practise. The second and third exercises can be practised for two minutes or 20 minutes, depending on how much time you have.

Exercise 1: Meditation for relaxation and sleep

Find somewhere comfortable to sit or lie and feel yourself relaxing. Become aware of your breath flowing in and out. Feel the cool air as you inhale. Feel the warm air as you exhale. Notice your abdomen or chest rise and fall with each breath. You may feel your eyes about to ... blink ...

Feel the clothing against your skin as you relax ... Notice any pressure on your body from whatever you are lying or sitting on, or the pressure of your shoes or the floor against your feet ... Feel the temperature of the air ... There may be sounds in the background. Let them just fade away as you focus on your breathing.

If you are ready, take a deep breath in ... breathing all the way in ... and hold that breath for a moment ... Exhale slowly as you relax your entire body... completely let go ... Relax all the little muscles around your eyes.

Completely and totally relaxed ... recall how relaxed you have felt in the past when you are falling asleep. Maybe you've had a really long day and you are so tired ... you're so relaxed ... unwind ... and it's so good to just let go ... Go ahead and yawn if you feel like it ... That's right ... so completely and totally relaxed ... Let go and unwind as you allow the relaxation to flow from your eyes ... all the way out over your face ... Just relax and let go of any tension as you prepare to sleep now ...

This is your time to sleep, so let that feeling of relaxation flow through your whole being ... tranquil ... calm ... In every moment that passes, allow that relaxation to deepen. Allow the relaxation to flow down from your head ... down through your throat as you swallow ... and the relaxation continues to flow down over the back of your neck and your shoulders as you just let go ... they just flop ... The relaxation continues flowing down through your arms ... deeply relaxing ... all the way down ... sleepier and sleepier ... eyelids becoming heavy ... maybe blinking several times, or not, continuing to become more and more relaxed and sleepy ... maybe yawning again ... Maybe your eyes are watering ... As you blink again ... allow your arms to become soft and loose like those of a rag doll, totally floppy, let them flop now ... even your hands and fingers relax ... you are so deeply relaxed ...

Let any stress in your back just dissolve ... any tension just dissolves like steam drifting from a teapot ... Relax all the muscles in your back now ... Bring your awareness to the front of your chest ... let your chest relax ... as you allow the feeling to flow down to your waist and abdomen and into your buttocks ... and your thighs ... the front of your legs ... and the back of your legs ... soft and loose ... Imagine your legs are like a big bag full of loose rubber bands ... letting go ... relax your shins and calves ... becoming so relaxed ... so completely and totally relaxed ... you realise this is now your time to deeply relax ... let that relaxation flow all the way down to your ankles ... your feet, and toes ... just letting go ... almost magically you feel deeply and completely relaxed ...

If you are doing this exercise during the day, you may want to take some deep breaths at the end of the exercise to re-energise yourself. If it is late at night and you are ready to sleep, let your eyes close and repeat in your mind the words 'sleep now' with every outward breath as you allow yourself to drift off into a deep, natural sleep.

Note: Once you are familiar with this exercise, you may like to find a quiet place and run through the entire process with your eyes closed.

The next exercise is an extremely relaxing chi kung meditation that can be practised anywhere at any time. In this exercise, you will focus on the meditation point referred to as the lower *dan tien*—which translates loosely as 'elixir field' or 'centre of being'. In Japanese culture, this point is referred to as the *hara* or 'second mind'. This point also corresponds to the navel *chakra*, 'wheel of light', which is known in yoga as the area where *prana* (life force—similar to chi) radiates out to the rest of the body.

The dan tien is located in the abdomen, approximately three finger widths below the navel and around two to three centimetres in from that point. When you centre your mind on this point, you can calm your thoughts and control your emotions. The point also relates to energy, focus and willpower.

Exercise 2: Meditating on one point

Find a comfortable position either standing, sitting or lying down. Relax your entire body. Let your shoulders drop and feel your breath flowing in and out. Once you are relaxed, shift all your awareness to the point just below your navel … allow your abdomen to rise and fall with every breath as you focus on that point just below the navel … As your abdomen rises and falls with every breath … as your breath flows in and out … focus on the point just below your navel.

You may want to slightly tense your lower abdomen at first. Relax the tension by half as you continue to focus on the point just below the navel. Continue to reduce the tension in your abdomen until it is ever so slight. The feeling can be more of an awareness. Your mind is now focused on your dan tien point.

If your eyes are not already closed, go ahead and close them. Continue to breathe into the point below the navel.

Note: Once you are familiar with this exercise, you may like to include a visualisation—for example, seeing a coloured light in your mind's eye, or sparkling energy flowing to the dan tien and filling up like a well or a spring.

Exercise 3, which involves meditating on two points, is a deeply relaxing chi kung meditation. In this exercise, you will focus on two main meditation points. The first point is the dan tien, which we covered in the previous exercise. The second point is known as the *ming men* point—which translates as 'doorway of life' or 'gate of power'.

The ming men point is found directly opposite your navel in the small of your back between your kidneys. You can find this point by drawing an invisible line from your navel around to the middle of your back between your kidneys. This exercise can also be used to increase willpower.

Exercise 3: Meditating on two points

Commence the meditation by finding a comfortable position in which to sit or lie down comfortably. As you feel your breathing flow in and out, focus all your attention on your dan tien point (lower abdomen). For a few breaths, allow your mind to focus on the chi in your body flowing to this area. Breathe into the dan tien and feel the lower abdomen filling up with chi ... As you inhale and exhale, continue to let this point fill up with chi.

Shift your awareness to the ming men point (directly opposite the navel on your back). Direct all your awareness to this point between the kidneys in the small of the back ... Breathe into this area and feel that area filling up with chi ... As you inhale and exhale, continue to let that point on the back fill up with chi ...

In a moment, you will begin to shift your awareness for one full breath in and out to the dan tien point, followed by one full breath in and out to the ming men point.

Go ahead and shift your awareness to the dan tien and take one full breath in and out. Then shift your awareness back to the ming men point for one full breath in and out. Continue to alternate from the front point to the back point, taking one full breath in and out at each point. When you are ready, close your eyes and continue alternating between the back point and the front point for as long as you feel comfortable.

Note: You could visualise sparkling energy or light flowing between the two points. After practice, you may begin to feel the chi flowing between the points.

Notice how calm you feel after doing this for only a few minutes.

DAY 1

Welcome to Day 1 of your Think Quit Seven-Day Preparation Program. What you learn in each daily session is aimed at preparing and arming you with the tools and strategies you need to become smoke-free forever. If you haven't already downloaded your bonus audio session, go to page 8 for instructions.

It is vital that you fill in your seven-day smoking diary in the back of the book, including every single cigarette, every day for the seven days of the preparation program. If you fail to do this, at the end of seven days I will ask you to restart at Day 1. Full commitment is needed. You do not have to make it a long narrative; you simply have to note the circumstances as instructed in the previous chapter. As a reminder:

- Record the number of the cigarette for that day and the time you smoked it.
- Note what triggered or caused you to need the cigarette.

- Describe what you thought or felt before, during and after smoking each cigarette.
- After Day 1, you will fill in possible replacement strategies.

Make sure you carry a pen and this book with you at all times because it is vital that you write the necessary information down for the next seven days.

On Day 1, do everything you normally would, and remember as you fill in your smoking diary that you will be determining some of the action steps you will take to guarantee your success.

One of the great things about this program is that you will be able to use many of the skills in other areas of your life. The program is not only about giving up cigarettes, it is about taking control of your life. It is important for you to understand that, over the next seven days, a reasonable amount of mental conditioning will be taking place. There will be a degree of physical conditioning too—note here that I am not talking about harsh physical activity, such as one-handed push-ups or weight-lifting, nor will you be asked to run up and down sand hills (unless that is something you would like to do—it would certainly add to your fitness level!).

This is all about mental conditioning, about mentally and physically breaking the old patterns and habits while giving you tools and strategies for when it comes time for you to say: 'Yes, this is the day. I'm ready to do it!'

Habit replacement

This is the first in a series of habit-replacement exercises. Often people stop smoking then suddenly find they don't have anything to do with their hands, or they become bored or tense. For most people, the first few days are the most difficult and they are unsure about what to do or how to handle their cravings.

The planning you do now is extremely important for your success. A crucial key in overcoming a bad habit is to replace it with a good habit. The first exercise you will do is simple deep breathing. If you are able to do this outside or near an open window, on a balcony or verandah, in a park, at the beach, wherever you feel comfortable in the fresh air, it will be much better for you. However, even if you are in a room with no windows, that is OK too. You can still do the exercise and gain massive benefits.

Breathing exercises will be a major key to your success. Think what happens when you smoke a cigarette: the cigarette goes into your mouth, you light up and drag on the cigarette as you take a breath in, then breathe in a bit more as you draw the smoke deeper into your lungs. Perhaps you hold the smoke for a second before blowing out. Then you repeat the same process until you have finished the cigarette. Below is a short deep-breathing exercise that can be done anywhere. The more you practise, the more you oxygenate your body, and the more alive and energised you will feel. Read through the following and practise the habit-replacement exercise for about three minutes or ten breaths.

You can do this exercise standing, sitting or lying—all these positions are fine for practising the exercise.

Habit replacement deep-breathing exercise

Make sure you feel really comfortable. Go ahead now and completely relax your shoulders ... let your arms relax ... let your hands relax ... Imagine your neck is like the string of a balloon and your head is the balloon ... it is floating up as your spine elongates just a little ... Relax your entire body. Let it flop like a rag doll.

Now, slowly counting in your mind, inhale to the count of four ... hold for the count of two ... exhale for the count of four ... hold again for the count of two ... Continue repeating this for approximately ten full breaths. In the beginning, you may like to use your fingers to count all the way to ten.

- Breathe in for four.
- Hold for two.
- Breathe out for four.
- Hold for two.
- Repeat.

As you breathe in slowly through your nose, keep your chest and shoulders relaxed, let your abdomen rise with the breath in and fall when breathing out. You can exhale through your mouth or nose. If you like, you can close your eyes while you do the exercise. Repeat ten times.

Practise this deep-breathing exercise as many times as you can throughout the day. At a minimum, you would practise it ten times several times a day: in the morning, at lunchtime and again in the evening, although you may also like to practise it more—even every hour on the hour.

Your body craves fresh air

You have just practised that deep-breathing exercise ten times and it most likely took you around three minutes. The exercise is similar to your previous habit in that you breathe deeply when you smoke, but the difference here is that rather than inhaling foul, toxic chemicals into your lungs and flooding your body with poisons, you are putting more oxygen into your body. It is very important to take ten deep breaths at least three times a day, or more. When people breathe without paying attention to their breathing, they generally only take in one-third or less of their lung capacity and fail to exhale a lot of stale air. The stale air left in your lungs and the smoke you inhale combine in a way that is slowly poisoning you. Start breathing more deeply when you are not smoking, filling your lungs and your body with fresh oxygen. Enjoy breathing deeply as often as you can.

The deep-breathing exercises are just one of the habit-replacement strategies you will learn that will help you to easily overcome any cravings that you may have during those first few days or weeks. Keep reminding yourself: *The cravings will not last, shortly I will be smoke-free.*

Benefits of NOT smoking

Take some time to look back at the list of benefits you came up with in Chapter 10. Perhaps you've thought of some additional benefits of being smoke-free that hadn't occurred to you then. Write them down now:

_____

_____

_____

_____

_____

_____

_____

_____

_____

DAY 2

On Day 2, keep practising your deep-breathing exercises and remember to note down in your smoking diary every cigarette that you consume today, as well as the event and emotion that accompanied it. I trust that yesterday you meticulously filled in your diary. It is crucial that your diary is filled in as instructed, because the key to overcoming all the challenges you face lies in what you write down. If you had 20 cigarettes yesterday, and for some reason you only noted 15 of those cigarettes, I have to ask you to start again on Day 1 of the program. If you didn't note down every cigarette, it tells me that you are not 100 per cent committed. If you cannot note down 20 cigarettes when it only takes you ten or 20 seconds each time, then obviously you are not taking the whole thing seriously. Smoking addiction is a serious problem that needs serious action. This is not a joke!

This is a critical issue: you are poisoning yourself hour by hour, day by day, every time you light up a cigarette—and what's more, you know that!

If you didn't succeed in filling in our diary, you really need to go back to Day 1 and start again. I cannot emphasise enough how vital this is. If you follow and persevere with all the steps as instructed, you will be successful—in less than a week from now you will be a non-smoker.

If you did fill in everything yesterday, fantastic! You are on your way to good health and being smoke-free.

Limiting beliefs

The funny thing about smoking—and most problems in general—is that people hold on to their problem by continuously using 'negative self-talk'—for example, 'I can't stop smoking', 'I'm a smoker, I'll probably always be a smoker', 'Smoking helps me to relax.' Or you may tell yourself: 'Having a cigarette takes my mind off my problems and things I'm worried about', 'I'm more relaxed when I have a cigarette', 'Having a cigarette gives me more energy and helps me concentrate.'

Aren't concentration and increased energy a contradiction to taking your mind off things and relaxation? All these beliefs are really illusions that you have created for yourself, and they have become like prison bars. Each limiting belief and negative thought represents one of those prison bars, effectively incarcerating you in an invisible jail that you have created. Negative self-talk serves only to reinforce your problem. Let's face it, for many people who have tried to give up again and again, cigarettes are like a prison—a financial prison and a health prison. The aim of today's session is to chip away a little bit more of the problem, to loosen the grip you have on your beliefs, so that at the end of the seven days you will be ready to break out of your prison.

As each day passes this week, your desire for cigarettes will become less and less—in fact, you may even grow to hate cigarettes. The very fact that you are reading this right now means you are close to being ready to give up—you have had enough. As each day passes, you will begin to transform your habits by building yourself up with new habits and strategies and new ways of coping, whether that means coping with stress, work problems or relationship issues—whatever it may be, you will have all the skills you will need to stay smoke-free forever. My goal is to help you reach this goal. Your goal is to be a non-smoker—not for a day, not for a week, not for a year, but for the rest of your life.

Disconnecting triggers

By the end of the week, you will be able to disconnect every one of your triggers, whether it is having a cigarette while driving to work, walking to the station or bus stop, with coffee or alcohol, after something exciting has happened at work, if someone gave you a pat on the back, you were chatting on the phone, you were on a break, whatever it is. It is pointless for me to provide strategies for disconnecting a 'coffee trigger' if you don't drink coffee, or an alcohol 'disconnector' if you don't drink alcohol. As you smoke each cigarette throughout the day, be aware of each of these triggers. At the moment, having a cigarette may seem important to you but the fact is it is nothing more than a self-destructive habit. You are only fulfilling the nicotine craving. It is time to stop being an addict. The following section on values will help you to identify what really is important.

Values

What do you value most in your life? What is really important to you? Perhaps it is your family, your career, your car, your friends or personal growth—there are many areas of our lives that we value, and of course we value life itself.

What I would like you to do now is write down all the things that are most important to you in your life—about yourself, your life, the world around you, your environment. Include all areas of your life. When you write your list, make sure to write what actually *is* important, not what you want to be important. Dig deep—really think about your life.

What things are really important to you? Write them all down.

Values list

_____

_____

_____

_____

_____

_____

_____

_____

_____

_____

When you can't come up with anything more, reread your list and decide which ten things are the *most* important to you. Assign a priority to each one with 1 being the most important, 2 the next most important, and so on down to 10.

Rewrite the list here in order of priority, starting with your number 1 as the most important thing on your list and continuing all the way to 10.

1. _____

2. _____

3. _____

4. _____

5. _____

6. _____

7. _____

8. _____

9. _____

10. _____

Now review your list and see where you have placed health and fitness as a priority. Is it up there around number 1 or 2 or 3, or does it come in at a poor 4, 5 or 6? Is it even on your list at all? Next, think about how important your health and fitness have been to you over the last year, two years, five years and ten years. At a guess, while you may have been doing some sort of exercise and attempting to eat healthily—even super-healthily—how important could your health be to you if you are still smoking?

If health is right up there on your priority list, that's great, but if it isn't you need to get it up there. One key thing we will do this week is make sure that health and fitness are high on your list of the most important values. It truly is something that you should really value because, let's face it, if you don't have your health, what do you have? You could be surrounded by the best family and the best friends in the world, but if you don't have your health, what does it all mean? You could have a hundred million dollars in the bank, but if you don't have your health, what is that worth to you? If you end up with lung cancer, all the money in the world means nothing.

Your smoking enjoyment

Once again, you don't need to attempt to stop smoking today, or even cut back, unless you feel really motivated and increasingly repulsed by cigarettes. It is important that you stick to your normal routine, but what I would like you to do is think about what you enjoy the most every time you have a cigarette.

- Is it bringing the cigarette up to your lips?
- Is it the fact that you are doing something with your fingers and hands?
- Is it the enjoyment of the social interaction?
- Is it the taste?
- Is it that you feel energised by having the cigarette?
- Is it that you feel relaxed by having the cigarette?

Smoking is not a single habit, but a complex one: there are a number of things involved. What I would like you to consider is what you enjoy about smoking so that you can really start to think about all the possible things you are going to be able to do to replace those habits.

As you begin to place yourself under the microscope, notice what it is you enjoy about having that cigarette. Notice the different elements of the habits of smoking that you are repeating over and over.

BREATHING REMINDER

Throughout the day, make sure you practise your deep-breathing exercises: breathe in for the count of four, hold for two, out for four, hold for two. Practise this at least three times throughout the day. You may like to time how long it takes to smoke a cigarette and repeat the breathing exercise for the same time.

Chi kung visualisation: The Inner Smile

You are about to learn an extremely beneficial ancient Taoist chi kung visualisation session called 'the Inner Smile'. It is aimed at allowing the energy, the chi, to flow to different organs and parts of your body. This is important because it will help you to realise that you do have organs inside your body! A lot of the time we forget that our body consists of anything other than our external shell.

It is time to realise that what you have on the inside is important—in fact, it is more important than what is on the outside. You could lose a finger or an arm and still live, but lose your lungs, your heart, your kidneys or your liver and you are in big trouble. Begin to really think about your body. What is going on inside? Using the Inner Smile visualisation, you are going to smile at the one person who needs it the most—you. So often, we neglect ourselves; the Inner Smile gives you the opportunity to appreciate—and love—yourself.

Our mind and body are connected. With your mind you will direct chi to the different parts of your body that make up the magnificent machine which is you. The Inner Smile will relax and heal you, and help you to respect yourself and your body.

The Inner Smile meditation

Begin by sitting or lying down. In the beginning, you will obviously leave your eyes open. You could also have somebody read the script to you in a slow, relaxed tone. After learning this routine, you would practise with your eyes closed. When you are ready, focus on your breathing. Inhale quietly while repeating the word 'calm' in your mind, then exhale while repeating the word 'relax' to yourself. Allow your body to relax … completely let go …

Now imagine that you are standing in a beautiful place, a place that is special to you. You might be in a forest, on a beach, by a river, in a field or a beautiful garden. Imagine there is a mist in front of you and in the mist you see a person standing before you. As the mist clears, you recognise this person—maybe it is someone you love, a relative or a religious figure, or maybe you visualise an angel or being of light. This person or being is smiling at you … Feel the energy of the smile like sunshine warming you, feel the energy of the smile radiating into your eyes … and feel your own eyes begin to smile …

As the smiling energy and love in your eyes begin to well up and overflow, direct the chi, the energy, to flow down over your cheeks and jaw … feel your lips stretching as the corners of your mouth curl up and as you begin to smile … feel any tension in your jaw just melt away … Let the soothing energy flow down from your face to your neck and throat, and feel it streaming down into your heart, filling it with love … As you smile down to your heart, thank your heart for tirelessly pumping blood containing oxygen and nutrients to your body and feel the love and smiling energy in your heart overflow … and spread to your lungs … Thank your lungs for allowing you to breathe and tell your lungs that you love them and how much you appreciate them … Instead of trying to breathe, just be … let the air flow in and out naturally, lightly, calmly. Thank your lungs for allowing you to absorb fresh oxygen and sending that life-giving oxygen via your blood to the rest of your body.

Just below your rib cage on the right side is your liver. With so many functions, the liver is often referred to as the Wheel of Life. Your liver will be rejuvenated and healed as you thank it for removing toxins and processing food nutrients … Take a moment to let the smiling energy flow through your liver and then send your smiling energy into your kidneys, just below your rib cage on your back. Fill your kidneys with love as you smile at them, thanking them for filtering waste and toxic substances, and for circulating chi throughout your body. Allow your smile to flow on into your pancreas, which is behind your stomach, just above the navel … Thank your pancreas for secreting the enzymes responsible for digestion … Let the smiling energy flow into your spleen, just above your waist on the left side … Thank your spleen for removing ageing blood cells and for producing antibodies that strengthen your immune system … As you smile to all your internal organs, you are sending them chi, effectively cheering them up …

Bring your smile back to your eyes, and see and feel the healing mist once again … Allow your smile to flow down to your mouth … as you swallow, follow the smile all the way down with your awareness, on to your stomach … Thank your stomach for storing and then breaking down all the food you put into it every day … Continue to smile down through the small intestine, thanking your small intestine for doing such a great job of digesting food and absorbing the nutrients and vitamins, and thank your bowel for being the body's waste disposal system … As you smile and thank all these organs, the inner smile will revitalise and rejuvenate your body …

Allow your awareness to return to your eyes and fill them again with healing light, the chi, and allow the smile, the healing energy, to flow through every part of your body. Almost like a waterfall of tiny diamonds cascading down … and with each breath feel the energy flowing to every muscle, every bone every fibre of your being.

Take a few moments to visualise and feel the light flowing through your entire body.

By sending yourself smiling energy, fresh chi, you are showing your appreciation to those parts of you that may have been neglected in the past. When you approach each day with the inner smile, when you combine both your inner smile and your outer smile, your life will be more joyous and others will feel your joy and your love.

DAY 3

Welcome to Day 3. The most important thing you will do today
is continue to fill in your seven-day smoking diary. It is absolutely
crucial that you record every single cigarette you smoke with
100 per cent commitment. Today, also notice what thoughts you
have around other smokers. Be aware of what you are thinking
just before having a cigarette, during the cigarette and after the
cigarette. You may begin to notice that, day by day, it becomes
more difficult to smoke. You may feel your desire to smoke
beginning to wane.

Remember also to practise your deep-breathing exercise
throughout the day: breathe in for the count of four ... hold
for two ... out for four ... hold for two ... then repeat for three
minutes.

Habit replacement

Today I am going to talk about how important it is to replace a bad habit with a good habit. You were not born a smoker. Unlike breathing, drinking and eating, smoking is not a necessary part of life; rather, it is a habit and an addiction. If you have found it difficult to stop in the past, it is probably because you are addicted to the nicotine, as well as the habits you have formed. All habits can be changed.

The most effective way to change a bad habit is to replace it with a good habit. If you think about it, maybe when you first started smoking you only had a cigarette when you were at a party or with school friends. The situation doesn't really matter. Maybe you had a cigarette one day and then you didn't have a cigarette again for a day, two days or a week, or maybe you just smoked a few cigarettes occasionally, then gradually the habit became stronger and stronger. In those early days, it is likely you could control the habit and that you could have gone for long periods of time without having a cigarette and without even thinking about it. Up until now the habit has had control of you and your life. It is time for you to take back the control that cigarettes have taken away. There are so many things you can do to replace that habit, and there are so many good, healthy things to do that will allow you to replace the bad habit.

While you will have several main replacement strategies, such as deep breathing several times a day, sipping on water either through a straw or from a glass or bottle, walking around the block or up and down a hallway, or simply walking across the room and looking out a window, you are going to come up with a number of alternatives. The more options and choices you have, the more flexible you can be in any place or at any time, and the greater will be your chance of success.

The more weapons you have in your arsenal, the easier it will be for you. For example, if you like oranges, consider cutting one or two oranges into pieces each morning ready to eat through the day. Most people I have spoken to say it's hard to have an orange or orange juice and smoke a cigarette at the same time because they just don't go together. It's a bit like putting tomato sauce on ice-cream—it doesn't work.

Maybe you could try a green apple cut into quarters or whatever suits you. Make the alternatives easy. The last thing you want to do is start reaching for high-sugar or high-carbohydrate foods, because that is when the weight piles on. As mentioned, many people who go cold turkey make this mistake, hence the theory that if you stop smoking you put on weight. Of course, if you replace a bad habit with another bad habit—such as eating unhealthy food—you will put on weight. But if you follow the Think Quit strategies, this won't concern you. If you replace the bad habit with a good habit, like eating a quarter of an orange or apple, or taking ten deep breaths, or power walking up and down a hallway, or drinking a glass of chilled water or cup of herbal tea, then you won't put on weight.

If you like holding something in your hand, perhaps you could replace that aspect of the habit by holding a pen, filing your nails, squeezing a stress ball or getting a lump of plasticine and squeezing or playing with that. You could use a whole range of diversions to replace your bad habit with a good habit.

Your habits

I want you to begin to think about what areas of smoking are habitual for you. On the right-hand side of the page in your smoking diary, start listing all the habit replacement strategies you can think of. For example, you could have carrot sticks, celery sticks, cinnamon sticks or cucumber pieces chopped up in a bag and ready for any time you feel like a cigarette. You could have a small tub of low-fat yoghurt, and have a spoon or two of it during the day—only have a small amount each time. These are a few ideas to add to your strategy list.

Mentally begin to prepare yourself for when you actually quit and you have made the final decision to be smoke-free forever. These exercises are aimed at preparing you to fill your day with good habits. Another great habit that you may like to develop is drinking herbal tea or green tea. Green tea is especially good as it is full of antioxidants. With everything you have been doing to your body by smoking, wouldn't it be a good idea to increase the antioxidant power within your body? Wouldn't it be great if your body was stronger at fighting off illness? Wouldn't it be great if your body had greater ability to fight off cancer cells? You may know that we all have cancer cells inside us already, but a strong immune system destroys those cancer cells before they have a chance to multiply and cause problems. Green tea comes in a range of flavours, including mint, jasmine and citrus.

You could have herbal teas such as peppermint tea, which is a good aid to digestion, and in the evening chamomile tea for its soothing and relaxing properties. Or you might like to try herbal and fruit teas, such as lemon and ginger tea, which is great for an upset stomach. They are terrific at any time. Teas are great replacements and take about the same time—or even longer—to drink as it takes to smoke a cigarette. For a range of healing herbal teas visit www.thinkquit.com.au. (Make sure you avoid or reduce coffee, as in the early stages it is known to stimulate the desire for a cigarette.)

Imagine that if you felt like a cigarette during those first few days of cravings, all you had to do was drink a cup of herbal or green tea or a glass of water, or take a few deep breaths or eat a piece of green apple, or maybe run on the spot, or practise the breathing exercise.

Imagine that all you had to do was eat a carrot stick. It is up to you to figure out what works for you. You will only have to use the replacement strategies in the first days or weeks. What you will find is that, as time passes, in a day or a week you will forget that you ever smoked. You will forget to have any cravings—that may even happen on Q-Day. You may even forget to have some cigarettes in the lead-up to Q-Day. It is different for everybody. But you will forget to smoke.

Imagine how good it would be if you forgot to ever touch another cigarette again. This will be the case once you have reached your Q-Day or soon after. How good would it be if you didn't give smoking another thought? Well, it is my job to help you forget to be a smoker.

Imagine if you forgot to be stressed out.

Imagine if you forgot to be upset or aggravated by little things.

Is this possible? Absolutely!

Everything you are doing here is aimed at giving you control of your emotional state and at overcoming both the addiction and the habits associated with smoking. You will recondition your habits, recondition the way you think and recondition the way you act. You see, you are not really a smoker—smoking is only 'a behaviour', it is not you. Smoking is not who you are. It is important that you no longer identify yourself as a smoker.

Today, you may still have a cigarette or two or three—or however many you are still smoking at the moment. That is OK because in a few days:

You will be a *non-smoker*.

You will be *smoke-free*.

You will remain *smoke-free for the rest of your life.*

You will never touch another cigarette again.

I would like you now to take a moment and visualise yourself being smoke-free. Visualise yourself not needing a cigarette.

Imagine you are out there in the future three months from now, six months from now, maybe one year down the track, and you look back at this time with delight and joy, knowing:

You have been smoke-free for months.

You are no longer interested in cigarettes.

Smoking is a thing of the past.

The great thing is that when you finish this Seven-Day Preparation Program you will be ready to take control of your life. You will have no need for cigarettes. Start to think about all the activities you can use to replace smoking. Seriously consider all the options. There are so many available that you are only limited by your imagination when it comes to the variety of things you can do instead of smoking.

Remember that your life as a non-smoker will be all about making healthy choices. Go out there and begin to enjoy all the possible alternatives—begin to experiment and find out what you like. Is it green tea, is it herbal tea? Is it pieces of apple or orange? Is it a little bit of yoghurt with some nuts?

What is it you enjoy doing?

What is it you like the taste of?

What good habit will replace your bad habit?

Start practising today! The following habit-replacement visualisation will get you started and allow you to put pen to paper with some of your own solutions that will help you stop smoking.

Inner wisdom self-hypnosis

Find a place to sit or lie down and relax as you read through the following visualisation. When you are ready, let yourself relax. Get really, really comfortable, wriggling your body into a comfortable position. Feel a wave of relaxation flowing over your entire upper body as you completely relax.

Imagine you are standing on a beach, making your way down to the water's edge, and as you walk along the shoreline small waves gently lap the sand, in and out, and you realise you can breathe in time to the water. As the waves gently lap the shore you feel your breath flowing in, and as the tide flows out you exhale. You realise how important it is to breathe fresh air. You begin to realise that your lungs desire only fresh air … your lungs desire only fresh air… your lungs desire only fresh air.

As you walk further up the beach, you notice something sticking out of the sand at the water's edge. As you move closer, you realise it's a bottle with a cork in it, and inside the bottle there is a rolled-up scroll. Obviously you are curious, so you remove the cork, you shake the bottle until the paper comes out in your hand, you undo the string tie that's holding the rolled-up paper, and you unravel this scroll. The title reads 'Herein lies your solution', but the rest of the page is blank, and at your feet you notice a pencil on the sand. You take that pencil and, knowing that all the answers lie within you, you begin to write down the habit-replacement exercises, strategies and steps that will help you to build good, healthy habits to replace smoking. You realise that your body craves more water; your body craves fresh air; your body begins to crave fresh fruit and vegetables; you discover teas that you like; and you find yourself throughout the day beginning to choose all these healthy alternatives until they become a part of your everyday life as you prepare to be a free and happy non-smoker forever.

Feel free to write down your solutions in the space provided.

You feel your head nodding in agreement—'Yes, I can do this!' you say to yourself. Easily and effortlessly, you begin to crave more water, you begin to crave fresh air, you know it is only days until you never touch another cigarette again. As each day passes, you know you will become more disheartened and disgusted with cigarettes. You can no longer ignore the dangers to your health, you think more and act more in regard to all the healthy choices you can make to establish new habits. As each day passes, health becomes your top priority in life.

Count from one up to ten, bringing your awareness back into your body and beginning to move, feeling the energy returning to your whole body.

You are now more focused on the need to drink more water, to drink more green tea or herbal teas, to have more slices of fruit, to eat more vegetables. And you will now allow your mind to be more creative and come up with new, alternative habits. The more choices you have, the easier this will be.

| DAY 4

Continue to fill in your diary. Now, here's a fun little exercise. Find three non-smokers today and ask them why they don't smoke. Then tell them you are stopping and notice their reaction.

Today we are going to discover more activities you can do and more plans you can devise to replace the habit of smoking. This is one of the keys—and don't just assume that you will find the habit easy to replace, because some people do and some people don't—the great thing is that you know how to deal with it, and you know that the nicotine is leaving your system. A craving is the nicotine trying to get hold of you again, but you will not let it because you know the cigarettes no longer control you. Now you are in control of your life. You may begin to find that your desire to smoke decreases. Maybe you forget to procrastinate.

From today onwards, even as you continue to smoke, begin to confuse the habit. If you smoke inside your home, you could choose to not light up inside and go outside for a smoke. If you normally hold a cigarette in your right hand hold it in your left. If you normally smoke at a morning tea break, change the routine and smoke somewhere else or skip a cigarette and notice what effect that has on you. Skipping one cigarette won't kill you, and you could practise a replacement exercise instead. If you have a favourite place where you smoke, change it and start to break down the connections. If, when you smoke in public places, you ignore the looks or the holding of the breath of non-smokers as they rush past you in an attempt to not let the poison enter their bodies, instead take notice and feel disgusted too. If you normally smoke with a cup of coffee, maybe try a herbal or green tea or a fresh vegetable juice or orange juice instead, and wait ten minutes to light up. If you normally drive and light up as soon as you get in the car, have a smoke before you get in and drive without smoking. Do as many things differently as you can to wear down the old habits.

Today, when you fill in your smoking diary, in the space provided on the right of the page, continue to include the replacement alternatives you will use to overcome the cravings easily and effortlessly. You are mentally reprogramming yourself to replace the old habits with new habits. By writing them down rather than just thinking about them, you are strengthening your resolve. Let's face it, even if a craving does hit, it will only last for a few minutes and if you fill that time with drinking water, running on the spot or taking ten deep breaths, the time will pass quickly.

Here is a list of possible alternatives and strategies if and when you get any cravings. Check off the ones that will work for you and include any extras you can think of. Bring it on! Let a craving dare rear its ugly head! You will crush it!

Habit replacement strategies

Tick the strategies that you can imagine yourself using.

☐ Change your thinking.
☐ Breathing exercises.
☐ Repeat affirmations.
☐ Visualise a happy place.
☐ Drink water (maybe use a straw and take sips).
☐ Chi kung exercises like the dan tien breathing exercise on page 83.
☐ Yoga exercises.
☐ Drink juice (no added sugar).
☐ Walk across the room.

❑ Weed the garden.
❑ Eat an apple.
❑ Chew gum.
❑ Clean your teeth.
❑ Eat orange slices.
❑ Drink herbal tea.
❑ Drink green tea.
❑ Play with a stress ball.
❑ Run on the spot.
❑ Eat a carrot or celery stick.
❑ Eat a cinnamon stick.
❑ Eat a slice of cucumber.
❑ Chew on ginger.
❑ Phone a friend.
❑ Call the Quitline: 131 848.
❑ _____
❑ _____
❑ _____
❑ _____

For additional replacement strategies see pages 227–32.

Ten-count breathing exercise

With this yoga-style deep-breathing exercise, you breathe in for a count of ten and breathe out for ten. When you breathe, draw the breath in through your nose and let your abdomen expand as you inhale and at the same time relax your chest and shoulders. Towards the end of the breath, you could let your chest expand and even raise your shoulders up to get that last little bit of air in and completely fill your lungs with fresh air. As you exhale, slowly squeeze all the stale air out of your lungs.

Take a couple of minutes and have a practice run now: breathe in slowly while counting to ten. You will find that you need to breathe very slowly if you are going to reach ten before you reach your limit. If you take a quick, deep breath in, you will be lucky to count to five. Inhale very slowly and evenly through your nose: by the time you reach ten, your lungs will be completely filled with fresh air. If you believe you are going too fast while slowly counting to ten, hold your breath for a few counts until you reach ten.

When exhaling, count to ten as you very slowly breathe out. If you only reach six, seven or eight, again hold your breath until ten is reached and very slowly expel all the air through your nose or mouth. Repeat the cycle.

With practice, you will easily be able to inhale for the count of ten and exhale for the count of ten. If you time yourself, you will find that the process takes less than three minutes, so to get through three minutes of cravings you may only need to take three or four slow deep breaths.

Healthy distractions

Basically, what you are doing in this deep-breathing exercise is distracting yourself while taking deep breaths similar to your old habit, except this time you are only filling your lungs, and in turn your body, with fresh oxygen (and chi), not toxic chemical smoke.

Other replacement strategies could include eating sunflower or pumpkin seeds or a few raisins or sultanas. If you need to have something in your hand, get a pen or pencil and do some doodling so that you are doing something else with your mind and your fingers. As mentioned above, you could also play with a piece of plasticine or a stress ball.

If you drink a glass of water, try sipping it through a straw—by doing this, you are imitating the habit, but you are doing something healthy. You can also do the same thing with juices, like apple, orange or watermelon. If you have never had watermelon, rockmelon and honeydew melon juice combined, try it—it is the nectar of the gods, absolutely delicious. By using a straw, you are putting something in the shape of a cigarette into your mouth, and in a short period of time you will gradually or very quickly forget about cigarettes, and smoking will become a distant memory. You will soon begin to wonder, 'Why did I ever smoke in the first place?'

Having spent so many years doing damage to your body, it is time to start looking after yourself. It is time to start being responsible regarding your health and reverse the unhealthy path you have been on. The great thing is that the damage you have done to your body *can* be reversed. The moment you stop smoking, your body will start to repair and heal itself.

You may like to consider taking a multi-B vitamin and vitamin C if you don't already do so. One of the most common deficiencies worldwide is B9, and lack of it means a tendency towards depression, as does a lack of B3. Vitamin B6 makes serotonin, which you need for good sleep. Cigarettes, caffeine and alcohol all interfere with serotonin production—the happy hormone. They also disrupt the amino acid tryptophan, which is required for the production of serotonin.

THE INFLUENCE OF SEROTONIN

The relaxation exercises you are learning, along with the breathing exercises and the chi kung exercises, all help increase levels of serotonin in your brain. This in turn makes you feel better. Serotonin is a hormone that affects your emotions, behaviour, mood and appetite, and assists you in getting a good night's sleep. So when it comes to stopping smoking, the more balanced your serotonin levels the better you'll feel. You can also increase serotonin levels with light therapy, so on top of practising your breathing exercises and relaxation, be sure to get a dose of sunlight every day if possible.

The most important thing you can do is change your thinking, your attitude and your focus. Rather than focusing on what you can't have and what you don't want, instead focus on what you do want—all the alternatives.

Rather than thinking, 'Oh, I am so stressed, I need a cigarette to relax', consider your alternatives—deep-breathing exercises, stretching to reduce tension, taking a warm bath, going for a walk in the park, squeezing a stress ball, or practising chi kung or yoga. There are great chi kung exercises a little later in the chapter, aimed at relaxation and rejuvenation, which are suitable for any age. I promise that if you practise these simple exercises, you will feel calmer, more tranquil and relaxed.

Face reality

As you get closer to Q-Day, you really need to reinforce in your mind the dangers of smoking.

Ask yourself who has control if you're smoking. The answer, of course, is 'the nicotine'. How is your health being affected? How much money are you wasting? What you actually get in return for your money is *a small box of poison*.

If you are ever tempted to smoke, remind yourself of what is in a cigarette by looking at the picture below.

What are you smoking?

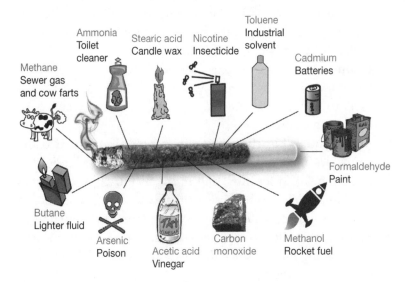

Ask yourself whether you would knowingly and happily put the following poisons into your body:

- **Arsenic**, a by-product of smelter dust from copper, gold and lead smelters. Known as the king of poisons, it is used in the making of lead bullets as well as in pesticides.
- **Benzopyrene**, a volatile substance that causes mutations in lung cells, leading to cancer, and induces vitamin A deficiency, leading to emphysema.
- **Formaldehyde**, a powerful substance used in making paints, explosives and disinfectant, which is also used to preserve body parts for medical science and in gas form can cause irritation

of eyes, nose, mouth, respiratory and gastrointestinal tracts, and the central nervous system.

- **Lead**, which has a cumulative effect on every organ in the body, including bones and teeth, along with the immune and reproductive systems. Lead poisoning can result in a variety of conditions, including impairment to the nervous system, as well as liver and kidney damage.
- **Polonium**, a highly toxic radioactive element used as a neutron trigger for nuclear weapons. It is the same poison used to kill former Russian spy Alexander Litvinenko in London in 2006.
- **Ammonium bicarbonate** and **ammonium hydroxide**, which are used in various cleaning agents, fire extinguisher compounds and fertiliser, and in the manufacture of plastics and rubber. They can cause irritation to the skin, eyes and respiratory tract, with increased values found in liver failure.
- **Phosphoric acid**, a component of rust remover and commercial cleaning products that dissolves tooth enamel and leaches calcium from the bones.

The list goes on and on—there are hundreds of additives. If you need reminding of the full list of approved additives refer to the list on page 38.

You would be excused for thinking you are getting a raw deal, and let's not forget the serious health risks—this list goes on and on too. It isn't really a good bargain, is it?

But wait—THAT'S NOT ALL! There's more! Smoking also gives you a racing heart, lingering colds, bronchitis and, especially after activity, shortness of breath; you get yellow skin, yellow fingernails, yellow teeth—and this is not a pretty lemon yellow, it is a brownish, yucky nicotine yellow. Smoking helps you to feel like a social outcast, keeps you dependent on an addictive substance, and takes away your control. It also has the ability to greatly increase your chances of dying a painful, ugly death. Cigarettes also give you smelly clothes, hair and skin, and if that's not enough they give you ashtray breath. *And you pay for all this!* It seems crazy, doesn't it?

Moving forward

During this week you will look enthusiastically towards the day when you become *smoke-free forever*. This is now only a few days away. This is the day you begin to turn back the hands of time and turn your health around. Even though your intention is to become smoke-free forever, initially your main focus will simply be on staying smoke-free one day at a time. Then one week at a time. Then one month at a time. Then you can just forget to ever smoke again.

The important thing today is to continue looking at all the possible ways you can replace your habit of smoking. Start to change your thinking. Every cigarette you have today is to be entered in your diary, along with a record of what you could do, what you would now prefer to do, instead—a healthy alternative.

Even while you are still smoking, it would be beneficial to commence some of your replacement strategies between each cigarette and start getting into the habit of eating a piece of an apple or orange, having a drink of water, running on the spot and deep breathing. Start implementing the new habit over the next few days until you are completely ready to become a *non-smoker*—until you are ready to become *smoke-free forever*.

The closer we get to Q-Day, the more you want to tune into your body and how you feel, as well as continuing to build some great habit-busting strategies. The more you practise your strategies, the easier it will be to stop smoking. The following exercises are to help you increase relaxation and tackle stress, as well as getting you to breathe more deeply.

The Tortoise pose

The Tortoise pose is an ancient chi kung exercise. The gentle stretching movements of the Tortoise pose decrease tension in the neck, shoulders and upper back. The flow of blood and chi is regulated, and moves more freely into the head and brain. Because of these benefits and the ability of the exercise to create a feeling of calm and well-being, the Tortoise pose is known as the longevity exercise.

Tortoise pose

Sit or stand in a relaxed natural position with your feet approximately shoulder width apart. (Once you know the exercise, you can practise with your eyes open or closed.) Form light fists with both hands and rest them on the front of your legs or hang them at your sides, thumb wrapped around the outside to prevent any chi escaping through the hands. Your shoulders should stay relaxed.

Inhale slowly as you look up towards the sky or ceiling, gently stretching the front of the neck as the back of your head moves towards the back of your neck. At the same time, slowly raise your shoulders as if you were trying to touch your ears with your shoulders.

Let your shoulders relax downwards as you exhale, and bring your chin towards your chest as you feel the back of your neck gently stretching.

Repeat the movement a minimum of three times. To reap the full benefits, practise a dozen repetitions.

The major benefit is gained through harmonising the movement with your breathing.

The best times to practise the Tortoise pose are upon rising in the morning and before going to bed at night. You can also practise the exercise whenever you feel tension in your shoulders or neck during the day.

Remember not to force the movement and to gradually increase your flexibility. The Tortoise pose can be practised anywhere at any time, and is one of the most beneficial of all the chi kung exercises.

Self-hypnosis

Many smokers I have known and helped to stop smoking over the years have been very confident people. They have been confident about their careers and in relationships, as well as in many other areas of their lives. But their failed attempts to give up the deadly weed have meant that their confidence has been shot down in flames, literally. The aim of this self-hypnosis session is to give you the confidence that you *can* and *will* stop smoking. There is nothing to fear because this time you will have a new mindset about smoking and the belief that you can and will stop.

Self-hypnosis session to build self-esteem and confidence

When you are ready, get into a really comfortable position, standing, lying or sitting down, and let go of any tension as you focus on your breathing. This is a time for you to let the world pass you by as you completely relax. Let all the muscles in your body soften as you allow the flow of relaxation to sweep down from the very top of your head to the tips of your toes.

Count backwards from 100, allowing your level of relaxation to double with each breath. As you go down from 100 to 99 to 98 to 97, let yourself fall totally and fully into a deep state of relaxation. Now say to yourself:

I have the ability to achieve anything I set my mind to. I am committed to improving my life, and I realise that as big as the world is, there is no other like me. I am a totally original, one in six billion individual. My life now revolves around being more confident as I believe in my own ability to achieve anything I set my mind to. As each day passes, from this moment on I grow in confidence. My self-worth grows stronger with every passing day. I will win at whatever I set my mind to. Every day in every way, my life is improving, I am now more confident, more in control, and I approach every situation with strength, enthusiasm and confidence. I am the master of my own destiny.

Nobody else thinks my thoughts and only I have the ability to change my thoughts. The problems in my life are only problems when I give them power, but when I change my focus, when I look for solutions, the problems don't have half the power I thought they did. I easily take control of every situation, with confidence. I meet any challenge with strength, with enthusiasm, with energy.

I welcome any challenge, because I know I have the confidence, the strength, the power, the passion to easily overcome all challenges, all obstacles, I easily turn mountains into molehills. I turn challenges into a springboard that propels me forward into the confident future that is now mine. In the past, there may have been times when I lacked the confidence to move forward to take control, but that was the past and the past has passed and I shall let it go, I just let it go. I am able to achieve anything I set my mind to. Anything is possible.

From this moment forward, my powerful, confident and positive thoughts will begin to crush the negative thoughts easily and effortlessly. Any time a negative or self-defeating thought dares raise its ugly head, I will crush it with confidence, with strength, with power, with passion, with vim, with vigour. My enthusiasm is my greatest asset. With my enthusiasm, I will trample over all obstacles and all challenges. My days will be filled with enthusiasm. I have enthusiasm for my health, fitness and well-being.

I hold my head high, as I roll my shoulders back. I stand tall, I breathe deeply, I smile because I have now stepped up to be counted. No longer will I hide behind a smokescreen, no longer will I hide behind excuses or feeble reasons, no longer will I take on board the negative influence of others, and no longer will I allow my own self-talk to influence me in a negative way. I am now more confident. I am an enthusiastic and self-confident winner.

Focus on your breathing as you count up from one to ten and become really aware of what is around you while focusing on increasing your health.

DAY 5

AFFIRMATIONS FOR DAY 5

Repeat the following affirmations over and over throughout Day 5. Make them your mantra for the day.

My health and well-being are the most important things in my life.

Health is now my number one priority.

Nothing is more important than my health.

Much of what we are doing over these seven days is arming and preparing you to have the strategies and tools in place to easily overcome your smoking addiction. Little by little, you are rewiring your brain with Think Quit to *not desire cigarettes*. And by the time you reach Q-Day, you will already be 90 per cent of the way there. You will have loosened your grip on the major problems such as limiting beliefs and fear of cravings so much that by the time you reach Q-Day everything will fall into place easily. You will be so ready. Everything practised throughout the week will have a cumulative effect and by the time you reach Q-Day it will all come together.

Remember to fill in your smoking diary today. You may discover as you do so that cigarettes are starting to repulse you.

Today we will look at the positive—and negative—effect of the people around you while you quit. There will be people who are only too willing to support you, but unfortunately you may also have your detractors. You will also learn some acupressure points to help you overcome cravings.

Support network

Let's talk now about setting up a *support network*.

If you enlist the support of one or more *quit buddies*—friends, workmates or family members who are also keen to see you rid yourself of a nasty habit—those first few days and weeks will be much easier. Their encouragement and support will help you stick to the plan. Let them know beforehand: 'This date will be my Q-Day and if it's OK with you, could I give you a quick call if I need support during the day?' You could also ask them to call you, especially in that first week or two, at different times of the day or night, to check on how you are going, to give you support and to make sure you stick to the decision to rid yourself of your nasty habit. It is always good to know that people are supporting you. The old saying 'Many hands make light work' is true in this instance.

Alternatively, if you would like to surprise everyone or you don't want to enlist family or friends to support you, you can call the Quitline on 131 848. The Quitline is open 24 hours a day and is only the cost of a local call from anywhere in Australia. Funded by the government and cancer organisations, it is there to help you and anyone who is quitting—whether it be going cold turkey or with patches, gum, hypnosis, books or any variety of programs. On the other end of the phone will be people who understand what you are going through and who are there to support you. Having the Quitline on call can make a huge difference to your ability to stick to your plan. They will give you different ideas on staying motivated with replacement strategies, and they even have a call-back service: at your request, they will call you at different times to check in, ask how you're going and whether you need any tips, or simply to see whether everything is OK. It is certainly a great service, and if you need to use it, then do it without hesitation. You might like to use the Quitline in addition to enlisting the help of friends and family. When you call, be sure to let them know you are using the Think Quit program.

Cigarettes and alcohol

For the first few weeks, it will be a good idea to avoid situations and environments where you are more likely to smoke—for example, if at the end of the week you usually go out for drinks and a few cigarettes with friends, it would be a good idea to avoid those situations. Remind yourself it won't be forever; it is just a temporary measure until you are in total control—and you know you are a non-smoker and nothing or no one will ever make you smoke again.

I've helped many people successfully quit in one-on-one sessions. In the early days in a few instances, two to four weeks after quitting, clients have called up and said, 'I went out to a party on Friday night, had quite a few drinks and guess what?' That's right, they had started smoking again. It is important to be aware because this can happen if you are not prepared in the first few weeks. When you have had a few drinks, you may become uninhibited, and your resolve, your desire, your commitment will often weaken. It would be a really good idea to avoid alcohol for these first few weeks. If you need additional support with cutting back on alcohol or stopping altogether, check out the resources at the back of the book.

Keep reminding yourself: 'A few weeks of resolve is in my best interest and will lead to a happier, healthier life when I get through this.'

Continue to follow the steps as outlined in this book and it will be easier than you think.

How to reject an offer

While you go through the process of stopping smoking, true friends will not put you down or try to sabotage your intention. Indeed, they will be proud of you, and you will be able to lead by example. As they watch you go through the process, they themselves may be inspired to give up the toxic, dirty habit, to quit smoking, to become a non-smoker and be smoke-free forever. However, you may find that some people will taunt you. They might say things like: 'Come on, you know you won't be able to quit forever, you might as well have one now.' This may be because they are smokers who are not ready to quit themselves. They are not able to make the commitment to do so, even though they know it is really bad for them. They do not want to be the one left smoking the poison on their own so they will attempt to drag you back in to the nicotine prison. You need to be really clear with those people that you are committed to quitting. Tell the other person that, while you realise that they are not yet ready to quit, you would appreciate it if they didn't try to sabotage your efforts.

Practise saying 'No thanks'

If somebody tries to tempt you to smoke knowing you have just stopped, they deserve to be hit with something that will make them think twice before offering you another one. Here are a few possible comebacks you can use if and when someone offers you a cigarette—some of them slightly cheeky. You may come up with some more of your own.

- 'No thanks, I'm no longer controlled by cigarettes.'
- 'No thanks, I'm no longer a choker, I'm a happy non-smoker.'
- 'No thanks, I've decided I don't want to end up with lung cancer, emphysema or gangrene, but don't let me stop you.'
- 'No thanks, I've decided I don't really like the taste of benzene, ammonia, hydrogen cyanide or acetone. Do you know that stuff is used in paint stripper, toilet cleaners and rat poison? Man, I must have had rocks in my head. Sorry, what were you saying?'
- 'No thanks, I'm saving up for a holiday and have worked out I have spent almost $3000 a year for the last 20 years on smoking. That's around $60,000 [or whatever it comes to] and for what? To fill my body with thousands of toxic carcino-genic chemicals. But it's a free world, so don't mind me.'
- 'I appreciate you wanting to poison me, but did you know one drop of nicotine would kill you really quickly? Luckily with cigarettes there are only small amounts poisoning you a little bit at a time.'
- 'No thanks, I would rather go and wrap my lips around the exhaust pipe of a car or go and suck on cow farts.'
- 'Did you know the World Health Organization estimates that, worldwide, close to four million people die each year from tobacco? Sorry, I missed what you were saying—did you ask me something?'
- 'I thought you knew I didn't smoke anymore—and it's not because of the ashtray breath, smelly hair and stinking clothes. It's not even the yellow stains on my teeth and fingers or the fact my skin is dehydrating and I'm ageing prematurely.

It doesn't even have anything to do with the constant coughing or the fact I have no sense of smell and run out of puff really quickly and am on a slow road to emphysema or lung cancer. It doesn't worry me that I have to go outside like a leper when I'm out at a restaurant. What really worries me is having an ugly falling-apart foot like that guy in the advertisement because I like my feet just the way they are.'

- 'No thanks, my therapist has told me to STOP' as you hold your hand out like a traffic cop. (Yell out the word 'STOP' and then show them this book.)

Here is some space to write down your own comeback line. This could be as simple as: 'I've finally decided to stop, so no thanks' or it could be one of the cheeky responses from above, your own clever response or a combination.

_____

_____

_____

_____

The more ways you have to relax, the less stressed and more in control you will be—which will ultimately help you to be smoke-free. It is great to have a specific word that makes you relax as well: revisit the simple relaxation exercise on page 75.

Tapping exercise
This exercise is great for reducing stress and energising your mind and body. Start at the top of your head and, with light fists, gently tap over the top of your scalp. Now, with your

fingertips, tap all over your face and continue working your way down over your jaw. Make light fists again and tap over your shoulders, arms, chest, lower back, abdomen, hips, buttocks and legs all the way down. This exercise should take around two minutes and helps to alleviate blocked energy and tension in the body.

Using a positive resource anchor

Let me ask you this: who is in control of your thinking? Who thinks your thoughts? And of course the answer is you. The fact is you can change your thoughts and with it your state in an instant. Nobody else thinks your thoughts, nobody else controls your thinking, you do your thinking. When you watch something on television or listen to something on the radio and you don't like what you're seeing or hearing, you can change the channel or station, can't you? Well, you can change your thoughts in much the same way.

Sometimes we begin to feel down. Maybe an event made us angry, sad, frustrated or disappointed. Our day is actually made up of a series of emotional states: we're happy, we're sad, we're enthusiastic, we're lethargic, we're energetic, we're tired, we're bored, we're overwhelmed, we feel great, we feel stressed, we're relaxed ... Each day can be this constant rollercoaster ride of emotions. Some days, the rollercoaster ride seems to take us down lower or slower, rather than up high and fast. Imagine if there was a tool that enabled you to switch off the bad feelings, switch off the negative thoughts, and change your state in an instant.

Well, guess what? We have just such a tool. Like flicking a light switch, this tool will allow you to change your state in an instant. You can turn a thought around or you can talk yourself out of thinking something negative: by using certain words or thoughts in your own mind, you can let go of the problem, or you can give the problem a different meaning. If something bad happens, you may take it on board and feel really bad about it, or you may choose to not take it on board, and not feel bad about it.

What you're going to learn is called 'using a positive resource anchor', and it's a fantastic tool that can help you put yourself into a positive state. Many great athletes, business people and even international leaders use this tool to get themselves into a positive frame of mind. You've seen boxers getting themselves 'in the zone' by listening to certain music, saying certain things to themselves—they're using 'anchors', particular phrases, songs and physical gestures, that allow them to change their state. It's like flicking a switch, and you actually can change your state in an _____.

Now, if you just said 'instant', then I've 'anchored' you with the idea to finish the sentence with 'instant'—that's an 'anchor'. A certain tone in a loved one's voice may 'anchor' us into a loved feeling, while other voices may grate on our nerves, almost like fingernails being scraped down a blackboard. Maybe even the very thought of fingernails being scraped down a blackboard makes your blood curdle.

Mentally, we are made up to a large degree by our memories. Mary had a _____; that's right—little lamb. Row, row, row your boat gently _____, merrily, merrily, merrily, merrily, _____. Where was that thought a moment ago? Buried in your unconscious mind. In the same way that these songs are memories buried in your unconscious, so too are the habits you will be busting over the coming days and weeks. You may have spent time learning nursery rhymes as a kid. As a smoker, you have spent time reinforcing the habit. Understanding a bit more about how your mind works will make stopping easier.

Certain smells are very powerful 'anchors' too. You might walk into a building and all of a sudden experience a flashback to primary school, a friend, a teacher, or a particular classroom. It just pops up. Why? Maybe it is a particular floor polish? If you think of apple pie, or a certain cake or fresh cookies, you may find yourself instantly back in the family kitchen as a child.

Songs are also very powerful 'anchors'. You can be feeling down but if your favourite song comes on the radio and you start singing along, either in your mind or out loud, you'll feel better. You might even feel like dancing. Your state has been changed in an _____. That's right—'instant'.

In a nutshell, an *anchor is a process of stimulation response*. This means that you are responding to a certain stimulus. That stimulus may be something you feel, hear, see or think. For example, if you're driving and see a red light, you automatically start to move your foot towards the brake. Once you combine the powerful 'resource anchor' with all the strategies and habit replacement exercises you already have in place, you will be unstoppable. You will be *smoke-free for the rest of your life*. You will have the tools to be a *non-smoker*.

Your mind is a powerful tool—a powerful weapon that, when used correctly, will allow you to achieve anything. We are transforming the 'mountain' of quitting smoking into a 'molehill', a pebble on the road over which you will step easily. Other challenges you face will also easily be overcome. You see, it's all about solutions. *Think Quit* is absolutely full to the brim of solutions for you to become *smoke-free for the rest of your life*.

Creating a positive resource anchor

Ask yourself: 'Would I like to be completely and totally in charge of my internal state at all times?' The reality is that you have the ability to be totally in charge of your own internal state. At any given moment, you choose the state you want to be in. If you need to be in a positive powerful state, you can be. If you need to be in a relaxed and calm state, you can be. You have within you all the resources you need to create success. The fact is that your day is made up of a series of anchors. You hear an alarm clock, and that immediately gets you out of bed. You may be about to cross at the lights and you hear that D D D D sound, and what happens? You start to cross. It's automatic.

Our days pretty much run on *automatic pilot*. Anchors come in many shapes or forms—they can be sounds, something visual or a touch. And we have both *positive* and *negative* anchors. An example of a negative anchor is seeing a group of co-workers heading for the door and knowing they are going for a cigarette. At an unconscious level, you're motivated to go with them. Or an unpleasant event happens during your day and you get stressed. What happens? You automatically reach for a cigarette. So an anchor is really a 'conditioned reflex'. Through conditioning, you react or respond to the stimulus in a certain way.

We are now going to begin to stack up a series of positive anchors. When you apply these anchors, you will change your state in an instant. First, you will remember times in your past when you have felt really happy, successful and confident. Then you will learn how to harness within you those past resources, those good feelings, to be called on when the need arises. To make this work, we are going to come up with a physical action that we will link to these powerful positive states. I'd recommend that your anchor be linked to one of two actions: either make a light fist with your non-dominant hand (so if you're right-handed, you'd make a light fist with your left hand), or touch your index finger and thumb, making a circle or teardrop shape.

Harnessing resources

There are three different points in time when you can establish your anchor, creating three levels.

First level: The first and most powerful moment to apply an anchor is when you are actually in the state. Say you have just seen something really funny—it is while you are laughing that you can begin to 'build' or 'stack' your anchor. Or you may have just achieved success in a certain area of your life—maybe you pulled off a great dinner party or a win at work, and you have been given a 'big wrap' or 'pat on the back'—and you feel really great, you feel successful. Right then and there, in the moment, 'stack' your anchor.

Second level: This is the level you will be practising today, and you'll find out how in a minute. It enables you to relive feelings from past events, drawing on times when you felt confident, successful or powerful.

Third level: This is for the small number of people who struggle to remember anything positive. This is what is called a 'limiting belief' (as discussed on Day 2). If, for any reason, you find that you have trouble recalling times when you were confident or strong, you will need to use the third level to create an anchor by imagining what it would feel like to be in a state of confidence or strength. Ask yourself:

- How would I be breathing?
- What would I be saying to myself?
- What would I be feeling?
- How would I be standing?

Once you are in the positive state, you would then apply the anchor you are about to learn.

Practising the following exercise will give you a tool that will allow you to change your state as quick as a 'snap of the fingers'.

Keys to anchoring

Here's a mnemonic to help you remember the steps in anchoring. Remember that the anchor's purpose is to help you turn around your state, so fittingly the mnemonic is ITURN. This stands for:

Intensity
Timing
Uniqueness
Replication
Number

1. *Intensity of the experience*: To make the experience more intense, I want you to float back, or imagine you are back, at that time, looking at the experience through your own eyes. Fully associate with the event.
2. *Timing of the anchor*: Make sure you apply the anchor at the peak of the experience or the memory. This is the moment you feel you are reliving the event.
3. *Uniqueness of the anchor*: The anchor needs to be a movement or physical gesture that feels unique to you. For example, if making a fist helps you to feel strong and confident, then use a light fist as your anchor. If you are a boxer and you are always making fists, you would not use a fist. It would be better to touch your thumb and index finger, forming a ring.
4. *Replication of the stimulus*: Your anchor needs to be duplicated in the same way each time. Once you decide how you are going to apply your anchor, make sure you always do it the same way. It is no good if your anchor is to touch your index finger

to the top of your thumb, then the next time you need the anchor you touch your index finger to the side of your thumb. It must be the same physical gesture each time.

5. *Number of times the exercise is repeated:* You will need to practise this exercise several times to build up your anchor until it becomes strong and powerful. What happens as you practise is that the memory, the stimulus, becomes neurologically linked and later you will find it easy to fire off your anchor when needed, thereby allowing yourself to change your state.

Now we're going to have a go at creating an anchor.

Test-drive your anchor

Recall a time when you were really relaxed. Maybe you were lying down watching TV, or lying on a beach or in a hammock, and you were completely relaxed. Maybe you were lying in a bath, a warm bath, and all your muscles were soft. Recall that time and re-create the scene in your mind's eye, from your own perspective, as you see what you saw, hear what you heard and feel the feelings of being completely relaxed. Double the relaxation. Relive the experience for about five to 15 seconds. Close your eyes and recall that time when you were *sooooo* relaxed.

Welcome back.

My guess is that you are now feeling a little bit more relaxed than you were 30 or 40 seconds ago. The secret to changing your mood is this: if you want to feel happy, simply remember a time when you felt happy. If you want to feel relaxed, remember a time when you felt relaxed. Of course, the flipside is that if you want to feel angry, recall something that made you angry. How many times do we see people relive an unpleasant or bad experience over and over again? They spend their whole day telling everyone they meet about what happened. Each time they repeat their story, they are anchoring themselves into that negative state again and again; their toxic thoughts can even infect you and trigger a similar bad experience you had.

How many times has someone related an unhappy tale to you and your response has been, 'The same thing happened to me when_____'? Along with this memory, you'll re-experience your own feelings of anger or sadness and you can lapse into a negative state. You walk away feeling down—unless, of course, you have your own positive resource anchor to call on, then you can simply listen, and be sympathetic and supportive. As the person walks away, anchor yourself into a positive state. Instead of feeling bad for no reason at all, you can choose to feel happy for no reason at all.

Finding your resource anchors

Read through the steps below and practise anchoring the states one by one. When you think you've got it, then stop reading and practise the exercise.

First, recall a vivid experience from your past that is relevant to the emotional state. As soon as you begin to enter the peak of that memory, you will apply your anchor—either the light fist or the index finger and thumb touching. The instant the memory begins to fade away, let go of your anchor. When you recall the vivid experience, it is important that you associate into the state: you will actually be looking through your own eyes. The more intense this state is, the more powerful the anchor.

As discussed above, if I ask you to remember a time when you were completely motivated, and you can only remember a time when you were a little bit motivated, you won't really be accessing a peak state of motivation. If you find it difficult to recall a vivid memory, then *imagine* how you would be breathing, how you would look, your posture and actions, what you'd be thinking about yourself if you were really motivated. Or you could imagine a movie or someone else's experience that would also represent that state.

Some people go into 'state' rather quickly, but for others it can take a little longer, so be patient and give it time if you need to. Once you have identified the event, hang on to the thought of that event. You must release the anchor the instant the memory begins to fade, once you begin to leave the peak state. This is important because you don't want a 'trailing emotion'; you want to be able to stay in that one particular emotional state.

You are going to anchor nine states in total:

- Motivation
- Enthusiasm
- Confidence
- Success
- Energy
- Power
- Passion
- Happiness
- Humour.

These states are all going to be stacked into that one little switch, your *anchor*, which will be either *the fist* or *the index finger touching the thumb*.

Step 1:   Recall the positive experience from your past.
Step 2:   Enter the state and associate into the memory by looking through your own eyes.

Step 3:   Apply your anchor as you relive the experience.

Step 4:   Hold the anchor on for five to 15 seconds and release.

To prepare, read through the 'states to anchor' list on page 138. As you look at each state—motivation, enthusiasm, confidence, success and so on—take a few moments to think of a particular time when you strongly experienced that state. You may like to write down these examples.

Now bear in mind as we go through each state that there may be a particular state that doesn't do anything for you. If that's the case, that's OK, just move on to the next state. On the other hand, there may be a state that we are not covering that you would like to include—in each case, think of a time when you experienced that feeling. Then feel the feelings, relive those feelings, and as soon as you begin to feel you are in the moment, apply your anchor by making a fist or touching your index finger to your thumb. Just after you reach the peak of the emotion, when the recollection begins to fade, let go of the anchor and return to the present moment.

Stacking your anchor

You are going to practise *stacking* your anchor again and again and again with all those positive states. Should you need it, you will be unstoppable when you apply that anchor.

You could also stack the anchor with each state *several times* to really strengthen it. For example, you may stack 'motivation' three or more times (i.e. with three or more different experiences). If energy is important to you, you could stack the 'energy' state several times by going through the exercise repeatedly, recalling different events from the past that involve the same positive state. You will stack the anchors one after another with each state taking approximately one minute, so the whole exercise should take around ten minutes. Let's get started!

Motivation

Remember a time when you were totally motivated to do something. Maybe you were going away on a trip, or preparing for a dinner party, moving house or going on holidays—it could be anything. Go back to that time now, go right back into that situation, and imagine you are floating down into your own body, you are looking through your own eyes as you associate into the memory. Float right down into your own body and see what you saw, hear what you heard, and feel the feelings of being totally motivated. You may like to close your eyes as you enter that state, apply your anchor—a fist, or a circle with your thumb and index finger—and now double the feelings of being totally and completely motivated and hold that anchor on.

As you relive that memory, remember how you were breathing. What were you thinking to yourself? Double those feelings again as you apply the anchor, and the instant the memory begins to fade, let go of the anchor, and when you are ready come back to the present.

Clear your mind.

What you're doing is linking those experiences with the action—the finger touching the thumb or the light fist—which creates a powerful anchor for you to call on when you need it.

Enthusiasm

Remember a time when you were totally enthusiastic, when you were filled with enthusiasm. Maybe you were enthusiastic about starting a new job or learning something new. Go back to that time, right back, and imagine you're floating down into your own body as you associate into the event. Then, as you relive the event and reach the peak, as you see what you saw, hear what you heard, and feel those feelings of total excitement, of enthusiasm, apply your anchor, and hold the anchor on, doubling those feelings of enthusiasm, again and again, as enthusiasm flows though your entire body. When the memory begins to fade, release the anchor and come back to now.

Clear your mind.

Confidence

Recall a time when you were totally filled with confidence. Maybe you knew something with total confidence or you knew you could not fail. As you go back to that specific time, associate into the memory. Float down into your body and see what you see, hear what you heard, and really feel the feelings of being totally confident. As you relive that event, apply your anchor, then double the feelings, until you feel confidence surging through every cell of your being, through every muscle, every fibre. You are completely and totally confident as you apply that anchor. When you are ready, when the memory begins to fade, release the anchor and let go, slowly returning to now.

Clear your mind.

Success

Recall a specific time when you were successful. Maybe you had just cooked a great meal or done well in a sporting event. Associate into the memory, see what you saw, hear what you heard, feel the feelings of being totally successful, and apply the anchor. How were you breathing, what were you feeling, what were you thinking? Associate with those feelings of success while doubling the feeling of success, letting it surge all the way through your body. The instant the feeling begins to fade, release your anchor and return to the present.

Clear your mind.

Energy

Recall a specific time when you were filled with energy, when you were totally energetic. It's possible that you had unlimited energy—maybe you had been given some good news and you were bouncing off the wall. Go right back to that time and associate into that memory, float down into your body and, as you apply the anchor, see what you saw, hear what you heard, really feel the feelings when you were totally filled with energy, and continue to apply your anchor as you double the feelings. When the memory begins to fade, let go of your anchor and in your own time come back to now.

Clear your mind.

Power

Recall a time when you felt really powerful or really strong. Maybe you lifted something you thought you couldn't, or maybe you were filled with mental strength. Go back to that time and, as you associate into that memory, float down into your body, apply the anchor, feel those feelings of being completely powerful. As you double those feelings, feel the strength surging through your body, filling you with power all the way to your very core, and right to the outer limits of yourself as you apply your anchor. Double the feelings of power, and when the memory begins to fade, let go of the anchor and come back to now.

Clear your mind.

Passion

Recall a time when you were filled with passion, either for something or to achieve something. Maybe you were really eager and obsessed in a positive way. As you go back to that specific time now, and as you associate into the memory, float down into your body and apply the anchor as you see what you saw, hear what you heard, and feel those feelings as you were totally filled with passion, and then double those feelings. When the state begins to fade away, let go of the anchor and return to now.

Clear your mind.

Happiness

Recall a time when you felt totally and completely happy. Maybe you were filled with joy and happiness about something as simple as a beautiful sunrise or sunset, or maybe the smile of a loved one. Go back to that specific time and associate into the memory, float down into your body as you apply your anchor. See what you saw, hear what you heard and feel the feelings of total happiness. Let your body feel good through every cell of your being until you are filled with happiness, then double those feelings of happiness, and double them again as you continue to see what you saw, hear what you heard, feel those feelings of complete happiness. When the state begins to fade, let go of the anchor and come back to now.

Clear your mind.

Humour

This is my favourite state. Recall a time when something funny happened and you were laughing. It could have been a funny movie, someone telling a joke, a funny incident, maybe somebody's pants split or they did something really silly—anything you found really humorous. As you begin smiling, go right back to that specific time and, as you associate into that memory, float down into your body and apply the anchor, hearing what you heard, seeing what you saw and feeling those feelings of almost falling down because you are laughing so hard. Allow those feelings of humour to surge through your body, and double them as you continue to apply your anchor. Double those feelings again, remembering what you were thinking to yourself, what people were saying … Feel the humour flowing through every cell of your being, and when you are ready let go of your anchor and come back to now.

Clear your mind.

Congratulations! You have anchored one event from each of the nine states. You now know how to apply an anchor. You could repeat this exercise several times or on a regular basis to strengthen and build up your anchor. From now on, any time in a peak moment when you are feeling loved, or when you are feeling happiness, confidence or motivation—whatever the feeling is—you can apply your anchor and continue to stack it up.

Altering states

Good feelings are one side of the coin; on the other side are those times you feel overwhelmed, saddened or depressed. This is when applying your anchor comes into play and you can change your state in an instant.

As an example, let's say someone is giving you a hard time or trying to convince you to have a cigarette. Then you can apply your anchor, smile and calmly say, 'No thank you, I'm a non-smoker'. As you say this, you could just smile with confidence, enthusiasm and energy as you hold that anchor on and nobody even knows you are doing it.

Remember that you can use the anchor a number of times when needed. If you are feeling a bit down or stressed out, fire off your anchor. If you have any doubts regarding your resolve to be smoke-free, fire off your anchor. In fact, it's a bit like a muscle—use it or lose it. You don't just stack it up once; that would be like having a few workouts at a gym then saying: 'Now I'm really strong I don't need to go back to the gym.' An anchoring exercise is something that you should practise over and over, continuing to stack the positive states, including the stacking of any other positive state that is important to you, such as love, tranquillity or joy. That way, if the need arises, you can use your anchor. Use it at times when you feel you need more control, a little more power over your life.

Remember that you can constantly build that anchor up, in the same way you would build up your muscles at a gym, or train for a swimming race by building up your speed and the number of laps you swim—it is the same with walking, breathing exercises or stretching, or whatever else you are doing to improve your life and health. You need to build up the anchor, the positive resource anchor that allows you to control your *state*. This technique is used by world leaders and sporting champions, and it will work for you. You carry it with you all the time, and if something happens to you during the day, you choose how to react to that event and you either act positively, using the anchor to take control, or you let the event or the emotion control you.

Blueprint for perfect health

The following self-hypnosis session is aimed at making your health the most important thing in your life. Let's face it, if health was the most important thing in your life, you simply would never touch another cigarette again. The session also aims to help you strengthen your body's own internal healer. This session could be repeated over and over to help create a mindset of health and vitality.

Do you realise that inside your body you have a *blueprint for perfect health*? Your body is a wonderful machine. It knows how to recover from trauma or illness. If you cut yourself, your body knows how to heal itself and you don't have to do anything. If you get a cold, your body heals itself with or without medication.

Obviously, one needs to create the ideal environment for healing to take place. If you have a wound and you let dirt and germs get into it, then your body has to struggle to heal the wound.

Deep within you, the *blueprint for perfect health* is constantly working to help your body recover, recuperate and rejuvenate itself. Every seven years, your body completely rebuilds itself. Every single cell, muscle and bone has regrown, replacing what was there before. Your body is in a constant state of healing, rejuvenation and repair. When you create an environment that lends itself to healing, you are in fact able to speed up the body's healing process. Use the following meditation to activate your body's own internal healer.

Healing meditation

Find yourself a position where you can sit or lie down and get really comfortable. You may like to remove your shoes and loosen any tight clothing, because this is your time to recuperate and rejuvenate—your time to tune into your body's *blueprint for perfect health*. You may like to play soothing, relaxing music in the background.

Allow your breath to flow in and out naturally. Don't 'try' to breathe, just allow your breath to move in and out gently and naturally. With each outward breath, double your relaxation so you become twice as relaxed. Continue this relaxation for the next little while. Let all the muscles in your body completely relax.

Imagine you are making your way along a track through a rainforest, noticing all the colours around you—rich greens and browns. You can smell the ozone, the fresh, clean air, and you can feel the earth beneath your feet as you take everything in. In the distance, you can hear what sounds like running water, and you make your way towards the water, eventually coming out into an opening where you see a beautiful, sparkling clear pool with a small arched waterfall flowing down into that pool …

The water is very inviting. It is shallow and very safe, so you decide to make your way into the water, which is only a little deeper than your shins. You lie there floating, not far from the waterfall, listening to the sound of running water, feeling the cool water beneath your back. You notice the bubbles formed by the waterfall coming up and under your back, gently massaging your back. You feel as if you are floating just above the water, and as you float you notice the canopy of the rainforest, glimpses of blue sky and beams of sunlight shining down through the treetops. In the distance, you see what appears to be a tiny star, and this tiny star slowly floats towards you. As it gets closer, you realise it is actually a small crystal rock, and it floats down to just above your body. All the beams of light throughout the rainforest shine on this crystal, joining to become one single light radiating towards you from the crystal.

Allow that beam of light to radiate into the part of your body that needs healing the most. Imagine that light pouring through you, filling that entire area of your body. As that light fills that part of your body, imagine that part of you becoming a tiny sun that gently expands to fill your whole body with white, brilliant, shining light that begins to sparkle like tiny diamonds through your entire body. Imagine the light expanding and growing, radiating through your body into every cell, every organ, every muscle, every bone, until you are completely filled with healing light. From the top of your head to the tips of your toes, your whole body is completely filled with light.

As the light fills your body, you feel healing taking place. You feel that healing energy deep and naturally within you, because you know your body has a blueprint for perfect health. You know that putting things into your body that will do your body harm is not good for you. You begin to make healthier choices, to eat more healthy foods, to take in more healthy fluids, and as you float there it is almost as if you are floating away, floating up in the air because you are so filled with the light. Imagine the light continuing to expand around your body until you become nothing more than a shell of light. Always remember, you are the light and the light is you.

Now imagine you are floating further up into the sky, higher into space, until you become one with the healing energy of the universe. You feel the energy flowing through you, cleansing and healing your body of any old illness, any old injuries, both on a physical level and an emotional level. You have that healing feeling flowing through every cell of your being. You become a river of light as you are connected to the universe.

Bringing the light back with you, return your awareness to your breathing. Counting up slowly from one to ten, gradually become more focused and more invigorated. You are fully present in your surroundings in the now.

| DAY 6

AFFIRMATIONS FOR DAY 6
Repeat the following affirmations over and over throughout
Day 6. Make them your mantra for the day.
  My confidence grows stronger every day.
  I face all challenges with confidence.
  I am more aware, more alive and more confident.

Be sure to fill in your smoking diary today, accurately and
completely.

Clear out all physical memories and connections

From Day 6, do not smoke inside your house. This will give
you two days to clear away everything that smells like smoke
or reminds you of cigarettes in preparation for life as a
non-smoker.

Throw away all ashtrays. Steam clean, shampoo or at the very
least deodorise carpets. Wash curtains and couches and deodorise
anything that smells like smoke. Eucalyptus spray is amazing.
It can be purchased at most large supermarkets. It has multiple
uses and is ideal for spraying anywhere that may smell smoky.

Nil Odour is also good for getting rid of unwanted smells. Wash walls down.

And don't just focus on your house: wash all your clothes and make sure your car ashtray is clean. Use your ashtray to collect change and notes that you may have otherwise spent on cigarettes. Every time your ashtray is full, transfer the money to a money box to save up for something special. You could also put some potpourri or lavender flowers in your car ashtray so there is a nice smell rather than the stale smell of old cigarette butts.

Remove all evidence. You could even pretend you are cleaning up after a crime scene because it is a crime scene in a way—a crime against your health. The fewer reminders you have, the better. It is time to get serious.

Now is the time for you to take control, to be in charge. You have been controlled for too long, you have been under a spell. You have used negative self-hypnosis to keep you smoking: 'I can't stop', 'It's too hard', 'The cravings will be unbearable', 'I tried before and failed', 'I'm not really addicted',' I can stop when I really want to', 'It helps me relax', 'It's not really as dangerous as they say', 'I knew someone who lived to 90 and they smoked every day', 'I'll stop one day when I'm ready', 'A coffee tastes better with a cigarette', 'A meal's not complete without a cigarette', 'Cigarettes are my friend' … STOP! It is all an illusion. None of those statements is true.

It is time to break that spell.

It is time for you to take charge of your life.

It is time for you to be in control again.

Using the techniques you learned yesterday for applying an anchor to an emotional state, I want you to remember successful moments from the past—happy or proud moments, enthusiastic moments and energetic moments. I want you to stand up, roll your shoulders back, breathe in deeply and think the thoughts and feel the feelings of success, happiness, confidence and being in control.

In order to be able to use your positive resource anchor when you need it—when you are feeling down or in a weak moment, when you need extra control, strength or power—it is important to build up your anchor. As discussed, the most effective time to build the anchor is in the moment. When you are experiencing a moment when you feel confident, successful, happy, that is the time to continue practising to build up your anchor.

Here is an example of how easy it is to build up your anchor. I want you to recall some incidents or episodes in which you felt confident, happy, loved, energetic, enthusiastic, in control or powerful. You might like to play some music as you're doing this, preferably an instrumental. Standing up, go through the feelings of each positive state and, as you are in the moment, feel in control and breathe that way, stand that way. When you reach the peak of the moment, apply your anchor, continuing to double the positive feelings—the feelings of strength, confidence and control—with each breath.

Make mental pictures of the successful moments, feel the good feelings of success, of happiness, of feeling confident, of being in control. Make as many pictures as you can, and as the feelings surge through your body, apply your anchor, and double the feelings, and double the feelings again, continuing until confidence, success and any other positive states surge through every part of your body.

You might like to imagine for a moment that you are a mountain, or maybe you are a mountain lion, a tiger, a panther. Picture yourself with the strength of a mountain or one of these animals, then double the feelings of strength. As you apply the anchor, double the feelings, then double them again as you remember successful, happy and confident moments from your life.

You now have a fantastic tool at your disposal whenever you need it to change your state, and you can change your state in an instant—it is as easy as switching on a light. So if at any time you are feeling a little down, apply your anchor and feel the surge of confidence, energy, power and love, feeling like you can have it all. All those different states will come surging through your body at the same time. You can repeat that again and again, or you could just pick one state. Let's say you are in a situation where you need to feel confident: just recall a specific time when you felt confident and go back into your body, look through your own eyes and re-experience the feelings you had when you felt the confidence surging through your body, then apply your anchor. If you constantly stack this up and make it powerful, when you need it—BAM—you can crush any negative state. You will be unstoppable!

The BAM effect

Here is another exercise that will allow you to crush a negative state instantly.

As you now know, your days are made up of a series of emotional states. All it can take is for someone to say something negative to you that in turn makes you feel negative or depressed. That state may last for ten seconds, ten minutes, ten hours or even longer, and what is happening is that you have become stuck in a negative state.

For a few moments you may feel really down, then you feel it's not that bad, and then you go on to use some negative self-talk and you feel really sad and bad again. You might then replay what you could have done or how you could have responded, then you feel a little better. Then you tell someone else about it and enter the negative state again. Everyone has experienced this at one time or another.

When you get into a negative state, it is up to you to break the pattern. To achieve this, you can do what is called a 'pattern interrupt'. The BAM effect allows you to do a pattern interrupt and change that state—in an instant.

Changing states

Sit down and make yourself comfortable. Then slouch forward, lean towards your right knee and look down at your right foot. Take on a depressed, sad posture and, while looking at your right foot, say out loud: 'I'm really happy to be here.'

My guess is that you did not sound very happy.

Now stand up straight and roll your shoulders back, inhale deeply and look up towards the ceiling. Give a big smile then say: 'I'm really depressed.'

Did you notice a difference? My guess is that this time you didn't sound depressed. There is a good chance that if you followed the instructions you actually sounded happy or even laughed.

This exercise demonstrates just how intimately your physiology and state of mind are connected. The way you hold your body affects your state of mind, which in turn affects the way you are feeling.

Sit down again and relax while I explain the BAM effect further. Do you recall *The Flintstones*, the modern Stone Age family, an old animated TV show that was later made into a movie? The show featured Wilma and Fred their little daughter, Pebbles, and of course Betty and Barney Rubble with their little fella, that's right—little Bam Bam. Remember how he would walk around with his club, and BAM, he would crush anything he didn't like, anything in front of him. This is what we are going to do: *change focus* and crush a negative state.

There is no need to sit around and be upset or anxious for hours unnecessarily. This doesn't mean there aren't times when it's appropriate to be sad, or times when we need to express anger, but it isn't healthy to allow a negative state to take over and control our lives. So, within reason, we can choose when to get out of such a state. We decide when to make the change in our focus, and that is what we are going to do—change focus. In a few moments, you will learn how you will be able to crush a negative state with a simple action while yelling the word 'BAM!'

I know that may seem strange and a little crazy, but it works. I do this exercise over the phone with executive officers of huge organisations in America, and I do it in one-on-one therapy sessions as well as with large groups. I can promise you that it does work. If you cannot do this exercise now because of where you are, then do it as soon as you get the chance. It is a fun exercise that empowers you.

Achieving the BAM effect

Now have a practice run at the BAM effect. Stand up, roll your shoulders back as you take a deep breath in, look up towards the ceiling, give a big smile and as you apply your anchor (either the fist, or the index finger and thumb touching), yell 'BAM!' as loudly as you can.

Sit down and have another practice run, this time standing up faster and shouting louder.

Sit down again. This time I want you to count to three, then jump up quickly, roll your shoulders back, take a deep breath in, look up towards the ceiling with a big smile and, as you apply your anchor, yell 'BAM!'

Repeat the exercise a few times, with gusto, putting in 100 per cent, and each time you will feel better and better. You will by now have changed focus and will be in a peak state—you will be in the moment of feeling good. Keep your anchor on for a few moments.

How do you feel after doing this exercise?

Obviously, if you are sitting around the dinner table with the family or at work and somebody annoys you, applying the BAM effect—jumping up and yelling out loud—could have somebody grabbing the phone and calling the guys in white coats to come and take you away. So in this case you would do an internal BAM. Remaining seated, you would minimise the physical actions but in your mind yell 'BAM!' while applying your anchor.

Now that you have practised the BAM effect exercise a few times, we will use the BAM to smash a negative state.

Smashing a negative state

In this exercise, you need to recall a negative event and then you will smash the negative state by using the BAM effect, combined with your positive resource anchor.

If you are still standing, sit down again, get comfortable and recall a past negative state—maybe someone did or said something to really annoy you. Recall that incident. Remember how it made you feel.

Count to three and jump up with a big breath in, shoulders back, standing tall, looking up and smiling as you apply your anchor and yell 'BAM!' Hold the anchor on.

Now how do you feel? Where is the annoyed state? Where is the negative state? That's right, it's gone. You BAMMED it! You smashed it!

BAM

With the BAM effect, you can 'interrupt the pattern' of the negative state. If you combine the BAM effect with applying your anchor, you will smash the negative state in an instant. That's how simple it is!

It is up to you to be in control of your state. Don't let the negative state control you. It is up to you to know where you are going, and to focus on what you want. As well as continuing to practise your resource anchor, each day remember to practise your breathing exercises, drink more water and continue to fill in your seven-day smoking diary. All of these things are important in preparing you to take control and become smoke-free.

SERENITY

If you want to feel calm and relaxed, the following ancient chi kung exercise is the ultimate natural relaxant. Many clients to whom I have taught this exercise claim that the Serenity chi kung exercise is the perfect natural tranquilliser for stress and tension. People who have had trouble sleeping use Serenity to get themselves to sleep. Because Q-Day is almost upon us, the need may arise over the coming days and weeks, so use this exercise to calm yourself down or help you sleep more deeply. Serenity will put you in a deep meditative state/trance within minutes.

When water is still, it is like a mirror.
The mind of the sage in repose
becomes the mirror of the universe,
the reflection of all creation.
—Chuang Tzu

Serenity exercise

Serenity is like a tranquilliser, and can very quickly put you into a state of deep relaxation. Allow yourself to imagine a feather floating lightly to the ground. This is Serenity, light and gentle. In the following exercise, as your movements become one with your breathing and your arms float up and down, the body's natural relaxants and feel-good chemicals will be released. Read the instructions on the following pages and refer to the photos below.

Begin by finding a comfortable sitting position with your back straight. Both feet should be flat on the ground. Place your hands on your lap with the palms facing up (Figure 1).

Keep your eyes open and inhale as your hands float up. The hands float up as if being drawn up by the breath (Figure 2).

When the hands reach chest level, turn the palms away from the body. Exhale as you push the hands forward. Lean forwards a little as you breathe out. Imagine you are expelling any stale energy or negativity or stress (Figure 3).

Turn the palms back towards you. Inhale as you draw the hands and positive energy inwards. Move back to your original upright body position (Figure 4).

Exhale as the hands float down and outward just past the thighs. Imagine your hands are like feathers floating to the ground (Figure 5).

Inhale as you turn the palms up and float the hands upwards to chest level. Smile slightly. Keep the palms facing up. Extend your hands forwards as you exhale, almost as though you are holding a tray. Lean into the move (Figure 6).

Inhale and move the body back to an upright position. At the same time, let your hands float down with the wrists crossed, right hand below the left (Figure 7).

Let the hands rest just below the navel. The middle knuckle of the middle finger of the left hand rests lightly in the same position of the right hand. Form an oval with the index fingers and thumbs (Figures 8 and 9).

Relax your shoulders, close your eyes and take three slow, long breaths through the nose. Focus your attention on the point just below your navel.

This is one complete sequence. After the three slow breaths, open your eyes and repeat the sequence. Repeat a minimum of five times or for as long as 30 minutes.

Key: Inhaling and exhaling should be slow, smooth and long, like drawing a thread through a needle.

Free from thought the mind is calm.

Self-esteem visualisation

Imagine that your body is an empty vessel like a bottle, and the top of this vessel that is you has an opening. I want you to imagine energy pouring in from the universe, the energy of confidence, self-esteem, motivation, enthusiasm and success. Imagine this now, pouring down, floating down through the top of your head. Like tiny diamonds sparkling, it becomes a river of light filling your body as it pours down, like liquid filling a bottle, from the top of your head to the tips of your toes until your whole body begins to overflow. Allow that confidence, that energy, that sparkling enthusiasm and energy to overflow down the outside of your body until you feel light, you feel confident, almost like you could fly or float away. You are so confident now, you are so filled with enthusiasm.

Think about the task you are about to undertake, your goal of being smoke-free. Picture yourself as a non-smoker, achieving that goal. See yourself filled with confidence, tackling every obstacle easily and effortlessly. Picture yourself with enthusiasm, moving ahead, moving forward. Picture yourself acting out all your replacement strategies. Know that you have an inner wisdom that you are now more self-confident, and your self-confidence grows with each passing day. Your self-esteem also grows with each passing day, and you know that within any problem lies the seed of a solution—you only need to look for it. When faced with a problem, you may like to repeat these phrases in your mind:

THERE ARE NO PROBLEMS, ONLY SOLUTIONS.
IT IS NOT WHAT HAPPENS, IT IS HOW I TAKE IT.
THERE ARE NO PROBLEMS, ONLY SOLUTIONS,
IT IS NOT WHAT HAPPENS, IT IS HOW I TAKE IT.

Remember, every moment you are making your own choice: have a cigarette or use a replacement strategy. From this moment forward, you will easily overcome your addiction with confidence, energy and enthusiasm, and you will now seal, deep within you, the thoughts and suggestions that are important to you.

Now, counting up from one to ten, you will become more aware, more alive, more focused and more confident. As you count upwards now, you are ready to face any challenges with confidence. Wriggle your body, move your head from side to side and have a big stretch.

In your own time, whenever you are ready, focus on being back in the room. You may like to sit for a moment and gather your thoughts and energy as you feel increasing confidence and enthusiasm surging through your body and mind.

It would be in your best interests to revise the whole series of exercises we've learnt, because in two days' time they will be the strategies, tools and techniques you will use to help you get through that first stage of being a non-smoker. As you do the exercises, you will notice more chi, more energy, flowing through your body and you will feel more powerful—better, in fact, than you have felt in a long time. When you practise the exercises, you will feel calmer, and you will be able to eliminate stress with greater ease. These are the exercises to practise:

1. Breathing exercise from Day 1: in for four, hold for two, out for four, hold for two
2. Inner smile from Day 2
3. Tortoise pose from Day 4
4. Positive resource anchor from Day 5
5. Today's BAM effect
6. Today's Serenity exercise.

This is it. Today and tomorrow are your last days of being a smoker. Be aware of what smoking has been doing to your body. Escaping from the nicotine prison is easy. It is staying out once you are free that is the biggest challenge for some people. Famed American author Mark Twain once said: 'Stopping smoking is the easiest thing in the world to do: I should know, I have done it a thousand times.'

Last year, a lady came to see me to learn how to stop smoking. She had just been told by her respiratory specialist that she had life-threatening emphysema and would be on an oxygen mask within five years if she didn't stop smoking. Her skin was grey. This lady knew that she was already quite unwell with a serious bone marrow condition, but this had not scared her as much as the threat of wearing the oxygen mask full time. Her only excuse to continue smoking was that 'It makes me feel calmer.' Six months later, she isn't wearing the dreaded mask and her bone condition is in remission.

Don't wait until you are threatened like this. STOP NOW! You can do this and be healthier. The time is nigh. You have had enough. You are not a quitter on life, but you will happily rid yourself of those toxic, sinister little sticks called cigarettes.

Remember, like the ads say, every cigarette is killing you.

Remember, every cigarette is poisoning you and those close to you.

It is time to stop.

It is time to be smoke-free.

It is time to be a non-smoker.

It is time to reverse the effects of smoking and regain your health.

Look forward to the fact that, the day after tomorrow, you will be a non-smoker and smoke-free forever.

DAY 7

Congratulations on making it to Day 7! Today is the day you will have your final cigarette. Tomorrow will be your first day as a non-smoker. From tomorrow, you are a non-smoker. In fact, when you go to bed tonight you will be a non-smoker.

Make sure you continue to enter every cigarette in your seven-day diary.

Stopping smoking is so easy a monkey can do it!

China is the number one cigarette-consuming nation in the world, with around 300 million smokers. It is estimated that 1.2 million Chinese die every year from smoking-related illness. Some visitors to Chinese zoos have found it amusing to give cigarettes to monkeys.

Unfortunately, like their human cousins, many of these animals have become addicted to them. Recently a chimpanzee named Ai Ai began smoking after the death of her first mate. With more traumatic events, when her second mate died and her daughter was taken to another zoo, Ai Ai demanded an ever-increasing number of cigarettes. Ai Ai was eventually able to kick the habit with the help of music therapy, regular exercise and special meals, including milk, banana and rice. Ai Ai listened to pop music through a Walkman to help get her through the withdrawals. The Xinhua newsagency said she 'squealed for cigarettes at the start but gradually forgot about them as her life became more colourful'.

How will you make your life more colourful?

Saying goodbye to the last cigarette

Arrivederci ashtray breath, *sayonara* stinging eyes, *ciao* to smoker's cough, *au revoir* to nicotine, *bis dann* wasted money, *adios* señor smoke, *yasou* yellow fingers, *hasta la vista* cigarettes, *bon voyage* worries about falling ill. Many people choose to simply smoke their last cigarette and be done with it. Others decide to hold a ceremony to say goodbye.

For such a long time, you have had cigarettes with you, through the good times and the bad. You believed they relaxed you when you were upset or stressed. Maybe you have spent more time with your cigarettes than with family members. Your cigarettes were like a friend—albeit one that was slowly poisoning you—a constant companion. But you now realise it is time to say goodbye. It is time to let them go. You have no need now for cigarettes and you will no longer poison yourself. There is nothing in a cigarette your body needs.

Here are some of the ways people have used to say goodbye. Some people do this alone, while others get supportive friends together to witness the ceremony.

- Hold a burial ceremony. Say as few or as many words as you like. You might just like to say 'Good riddance'.
- Hold a bonfire and throw any remaining cigarettes into the fire.
- Jump on the cigarettes until they are crushed, then throw them in the bin.
- You may like to break each cigarette in half and, with each broken cigarette, say goodbye to one of the side-effects of smoking, such as ashtray breath, coughs, running out of puff, etc.
- Throw them into a bucket of water, or throw them on the ground and hose them down.
- Crush them with your hands and throw them in the bin.

However you decide to say goodbye will be just right for you. Be firm and strong in your conviction to be smoke-free. Say goodbye with no intention of ever going back. This is final. Make a decision on how you would like to say goodbye and prepare to do it either tonight after your last cigarette or on the morning of Q-Day to celebrate your freedom from the nicotine monster.

Breaking the illusion

Earlier in this book, we talked about beliefs. You might hold some of the following beliefs: 'I am a smoker', 'When I jump in the car I need to have a cigarette', 'A coffee tastes better with a cigarette', 'I need to have a cigarette after eating'. All these beliefs are *conditioned habits*, and your bad habits are just an illusion: you know that there are millions of people who drive cars without a cigarette and they do it easily and effortlessly because they are non-smokers and they don't even think of having a cigarette. They may think thousands of other things, but certainly not about smoking cigarettes. Indeed, there are millions of people who experience stress without needing to reach for a cigarette. Again, as I said earlier, cigarettes actually increase your stress because they dehydrate your body and affect you in so many other adverse ways.

Over the last six days you have been preparing yourself to be smoke-free. You have learnt the tools, strategies and replacement exercises that you can easily use any time you are feeling stressed.

You have the choice to be smoke-free. After today, you will no longer be a prisoner in the nicotine jail you have built for yourself.

White handkerchief exercise

Even if you have done the white handkerchief exercise years ago, let's do it here now anyway.

Get a slightly damp white handkerchief or tissue. Light up a cigarette and, when exhaling, blow the smoke through the same spot each time. Now imagine you continue to smoke and the icky, brownish muck is multiplied 200,000 times. If you have smoked 20 cigarettes a day for 30 years than that is how much toxic muck you have put into your body.

With every drag of a cigarette, you are lining your lungs with blackish-brown sticky tar. The tar makes it difficult for your lungs to absorb oxygen. The tar gradually builds to the point where breathing becomes difficult.

You are ready to turn back the hands of time, to let your body start healing itself. Cigarette smoke is not meant to enter your body. It is toxic.

Negative anchor

If tomorrow morning you had a call from your best friend or favourite uncle and they told you they had just found out they had lung cancer from smoking, you would be pretty shocked. You might even think to yourself: 'I really should stop.'

Maybe you would, maybe you wouldn't. However, if you got to work and found out that one of your workmates and smoking buddies had suffered a stroke the previous night (obviously brought on by smoking), you would be starting to think more seriously about stopping. If by the end of the day you had a really bad flu—the worst flu you had ever had, with razor-blade sore throat, totally blocked nose, aches and pains, a massive headache, a constant cough and chest pains—you would definitely not want to light up. What if, being so sick, you went to the doctor and were told that you were at risk of developing emphysema if you did not stop smoking? Imagine that the doctor then told you that you were also increasing your chance of a heart attack by continuing to smoke. You would seriously think about why you should continue to smoke. I know if it were me I would be ready to stop there and then.

Then when you get home, imagine turning on the news to learn that somebody has been killed in a house fire started from a cigarette. Before going to bed that night, you hear about another friend who has had a heart attack, most likely brought on by smoking. Lying in bed, you listen to the radio, on which there is a representative from the Quitline talking about how the equivalent of a jumbo jet full of people die worldwide every 45 minutes, every day of the year, from preventable smoking-related illness.

You would want to stop.

You would be so emotionally knocked around by all this that you would *have* to stop. All the reasoning in the world would not keep you smoking. Your unconscious mind's highest prime directive is to preserve your body. That is why you keep getting the messages to stop. Your unconscious mind would take over and not let you touch another cigarette.

While all of these scenarios may have happened to you at some point, or you might have heard of such events, it is likely they did not happen all on the one day—if they did, you would have massive motivation to stop smoking, wouldn't you? You would never want to pick up another cigarette again.

We are now going to re-create these events in our minds and re-experience them so that we can use the negative motivation.

Remember practising the positive resource anchor on Day 5? This was all about utilising positive past experiences and their associated states to harness the states you need to be in control. Well, now we are going to undertake a similar process, but this time you will recall some negative events and link smoking to these.

Negative anchor 1

Step 1: Call to mind as many negative events that relate to smoking as you can. Examples might include health scares, illness or death of friends and other negatives such as stained skin, yellow teeth, ashtray breath and the messages on cigarette packets. List them in the space provided.

_____

_____

_____

_____

_____

_____

_____

_____

_____

_____

Step 2: Now run through each of the negative events in detail. Imagine you are looking through your own eyes as you relive each event. See what you saw, hear what you heard and feel the feelings associated with each negative event. Continue to repeat the events over and over, running them through your mind as quickly as possible while stacking the negative states one on top of the other. Keep looking at your negative list and make hundreds of pictures in your mind relating to all the negatives of smoking. Make the pictures bigger and brighter and more colourful. Bring the pictures to life, closer to yourself. As you feel repulsed by all of this, feel the negative emotional push to want to stop smoking. Keep repeating the process as quickly as possible and let all the images start to become part of one big ugly picture. Include the cigarette packet pictures with the gangrenous foot, the eye, rotten teeth, tar on the lungs, the red artery. You may include the negative messages you have seen a thousand times on the packets but have ignored in the past. Let everything become a series of images flashing through your mind as you feel the feelings of negativity and disgust.

Step 3: As soon as the negativity is peaking and feels totally devastating, I want you to bring to mind one of your smoking triggers. Notice how bad it feels to even consider a cigarette. Imagine a cigarette in front of you as you say in your mind, 'NO! I'm over smoking. I will never touch a cigarette again.' Feel the trigger being totally collapsed by the negative state. See yourself throwing the cigarettes away as you feel disgusted.

Note: You may need to repeat this process on some of your main triggers, although once for each trigger may be enough. Work your way through each smoking trigger and event as you smash them to smithereens. Keep repeating the process until you are totally disgusted by cigarettes and everything they stand for.

Negative anchor 2: Yuck, I'll never touch a cigarette again!

Imagine a plate piled high with the most disgusting substances you can imagine—for example, hot dripping tar, sweat, dandruff, cigarette butts, dog poo, toenail scrapings, mouldy fruit, used bandaids, toxic poisons like cleaning fluid and rat poison, or whatever most grosses you out. Imagine the plate is right in front of you and it is disgusting. Now put that plate out to the left. Imagine that in your right hand is a packet of cigarettes. Now, picture yourself emptying the packet of cigarettes on to the plate of muck. The muck is like quicksand and the cigarettes sink down into the plateful of muck. Imagine now you are dragging one of those disgusting poisonous cigarettes from the putrid muck. You bring it up towards your mouth, and as you do, the smell is disgusting. You feel like you are going to vomit. You want to throw it all away but you push on, putting the cigarette in your mouth. You are almost sick as you light up the cigarette and feel hot tar running down your throat. It is burning your throat, it is stinging, it stinks, it is disgusting and melts down your throat as the burning and stinging sensations double in intensity. You feel as if you could vomit as you throw the cigarette away and yell in your mind, 'YUCK, I'LL NEVER TOUCH A CIGARETTE AGAIN!'

You may choose to repeat this process several times until you are practically sickened by even the thought of a cigarette.

On stress

If you are feeling stressed, focus on ways to deal with the stress—for example, talk to a friend, have a hot bath, go for a walk, stretch, do deep-breathing exercises, lie down and read a book, or have a massage. Practise the Serenity chi kung exercise or the Tortoise pose. Drink some chamomile tea. You now have new choices. Remember that a cigarette does not reduce stress: all you would have done is distract yourself for a few minutes as well as fulfilling the nicotine craving. Now you realise that you can distract yourself in many other, positive ways.

Get excited by any cravings: this is the nicotine leaving your system and a last-ditch attempt by the nicotine monster to get you to commit a crime while on parole and have you thrown straight back in the big house with all the other offenders.

After today, you will never need to smoke again. Now that you know what you do about cigarettes, you are aware that you would be certifiably crazy to continue being a smoker. There may have been times when you've been a little mad or even silly, but not certifiably crazy.

It's all in your mind

Your attitude from now on needs to be that of a happy non-smoker. Remember that you are not missing out on anything: you have only created the illusion that you need cigarettes. Every cigarette you have is doing nothing more than fulfilling the craving brought on by the nicotine.

The earlier exercises in handling stress will have enabled you to understand one very important thing about your mind: you *choose* to feel the feelings you experience. You choose to be happy, sad, angry, or any other feelings you may have. How many times have you heard yourself say, 'They made me angry' or 'They made me sad'? But now you understand that you choose your feelings by taking on board the thoughts, actions or emotions of other people.

How often have you been somewhere and somebody has said something that you found offensive, while others were unconcerned by it? You may remember a time when the boss, a customer or an acquaintance said something to you or made a remark that you found upsetting; however, when you thought about it later you realised the same thing had been said to someone else and they just shrugged it off—how did they do that?

IT IS ABOUT LETTING GO.

When someone huffs and puffs and carries on in a negative way towards you, it is up to you to make the choice to *let that problem go*. It is only when you replay the event over and over in your mind that it becomes a problem. The very fact that we are alive means that our emotions go up and down, we have good and bad days—this is just part of life, but it is our choice how long the bad feeling lasts. Practise the exercises in this book over and over until it becomes second nature for you to let go of stress and worries.

Of course, there will be times when you have to deal with genuinely difficult and upsetting issues. However, you don't have to let yourself get weighed down by them. There is no need to hang on to negative events from the past, and the emotions connected to those events, such as anger, sadness, fear, hurt, guilt or conflict. Holding on to these negative emotions doesn't help you in any way.

Below is another exercise to enable you to enter a calm state at any time you wish.

Becoming one with everything around you

The state you will practise in the following exercise is called 'Looking through', and it utilises your peripheral vision. It is a very tranquil state in which you become one with everything around you. This is another state that many sports people use. It is also popular with Zen monks and in particular martial arts practitioners. This is the state of awareness a Shaolin monk or Samurai enters when in combat, as it allows you to *get in the zone* to a place where there are no problems or worrying thoughts.

The 'looking through' exercise can be combined with some of the chi kung moving and breathing exercises, or simply with relaxing.

'Looking through' exercise

Sit down, get comfortable and relax, keeping your eyes open. Let your shoulders relax and your arms hang loose, letting your breath flow easily in and out.

Looking directly ahead at the opposite wall, or into the distance not too far away, choose one point to focus on—it could be a mark on the wall, part of a painting, a brick, part of a tree, anything on which you can comfortably focus.

As you sit there completely relaxed, stare at that spot and focus all your attention and energy into that one point. Continue to relax, and as you stare at that spot allow your eyes to soften just a little. Without moving your eyes, let your vision expand to take in the entire wall, or the entire scene in front of you, expanding your vision to encompass the full periphery.

Continue to look at that spot and at the same time calmly notice that you can see the floor or the ground in front of you, and you can see the ceiling or the sky. Notice that you can also see to the left and right without moving your eyes. Still not moving your eyes from that spot, allow your vision to expand all the way out—maybe you can even see your own body by now.

As you continue to relax and look at the spot, become one with everything in the room or place where you are sitting. Allow your awareness to continue expanding all the way around. I know that you physically can't see 360 degrees, but allow your awareness to expand beyond 180 degrees, until you feel what you see, see what you feel, as you become one with everything around you and allow your vision to take in everything, so that you can see everything, feel everything. As you continue to see everything at once and feel everything at once, hold that peripheral vision, hold on to the feeling. Remain in a state of peripheral vision as you look through and become one with everything. And here is the amazing thing about looking through: it is practically impossible to hold a negative thought or problem in your mind while maintaining this calm, centred state.

While continuing to look through, ask yourself: 'What is my problem?' While holding on to that vision, you may find it difficult—even impossible—to hold on to a problem in your mind. If a problem arises so will a solution.

Notice how relaxed you are. Let everything relax and keep hold of that vision, as you *become one with everything*.

Now relax and refocus your eyes, returning to normal.

Think about what just happened. Did you find it hard to think of a problem while you were actually in that state? If you did, well done! If not, you may need to practise the exercise a number of times and really hold on to the feeling of expanded awareness.

So, if you were to switch on that peripheral vision while applying your positive resource anchor, while doing the BAM effect, while sipping on some water between taking ten deep breaths, and repeating 'The new me is smoke-free', you will be *unstoppable*. OK, maybe you won't do all of those things at once, but you could easily do the breathing exercise while maintaining the peripheral vision, then follow that with ten sips of water or whatever else works for you.

As discussed, it is important that you customise the relaxation techniques, habit-replacement exercises and craving-busting strategies to suit you. What you are doing with these exercises is empowering yourself. The more flexible you are with your attitude, the more choices you have. It is up to you to take the suggestions on board and make them your own, to own the exercises. It is up to you to make that commitment to yourself for your health.

'The new me is smoke-free' breathing exercise
As you breathe in, say: 'THE NEW ME'. Then as you breathe out, say: 'IS SMOKE-FREE.' Repeat that affirmation over and over, ten times, with ten slow deep breaths.

In: THE NEW ME …

Out: IS SMOKE-FREE.

If someone offers you a cigarette, refuse politely and repeat your affirmation in your mind:

THE NEW ME IS SMOKE-FREE.

Whenever you see someone smoking you could think to yourself:

THE NEW ME IS SMOKE-FREE.

THE NEW ME IS SMOKE-FREE.

Keep repeating this phrase and feel happy about it. Let go of any bad feelings and *choose to feel happy for no reason at all*.

The fact is that your decision to *become smoke-free—to be a non-smoker*—is the right one. You have probably wanted to do this for a long time and have been hiding from reality and pretending that cigarettes won't do you any harm, while deep down inside you know that they are slowly killing you.

Think of the immeasurable pleasure, the strength, the control over your life you will have as a *non-smoker*. Think of the success that will follow simply because you know that by stopping smoking you can succeed in other areas of your life that you may have neglected. Think of how many holidays you can enjoy with the money you will have saved. Think of being physically stronger and healthier. Think of all the extra time you'll have.

Extra time and money

Now that you are smoke-free, you will have extra time and money to pursue pleasurable pastimes. Let's now think of an activity you can take up to fill in that extra time, something that will benefit you and that you will enjoy. Here are some suggestions—feel free to add your own:

- Commit to daily breathing exercises.
- Join a gym and make a commitment to go regularly.
- Get a personal trainer.
- Go for daily walks.
- Take up yoga, tai chi, chi kung or Pilates.
- Start an art class or a TAFE course.
- Take up pottery or woodworking.
- Try swimming or water aerobics at your local pool.
- Take line-dancing, Latin or salsa dancing classes.
- Try a sport such as tennis or golf.
- Take up a martial art such as boxing, ju jutsu or karate.

These are just a few ideas for you to think about—no doubt there is something you have always wanted to do but for which you never had the money, time or motivation when the old you was sitting around having a cigarette. The *new you* is interested in other things, so get moving—and enjoy your life.

We all suffer adversity in our lives—some things are harder and more serious than others—and you will have heard stories about people who triumphed over tragedy, beat the odds and conquered their problems. Rather than focus on the things you can't do, focus on the things you can do. Focus on the choices you have—in your case, you need to think about all the alternatives to smoking as you replace the old habit.

Next, you will learn how to rid yourself of the limiting beliefs that have kept you smoking.

The seven-day smoking diary

We will now get to utilise what you have recorded in your daily smoking diary.

If, for any reason, you didn't include every cigarette in your diary as instructed, accompanied by notes about the triggering event and your state of mind, you will need to start the seven days again and take it seriously this time.

You must be totally committed, not just 80 or 90 per cent committed. Even 99 per cent is not good enough. Only 100 per cent will get you the results you are after.

If you are reading on, presumably you have completed your seven-day smoking diary with total accuracy.

Recognising limiting beliefs and smoking associations

Go back now to Day 1 of your seven-day diary. Looking at each day, identify any times or reasons for smoking that were similar.

Was it when you got out of bed, with your first coffee or after each meal? Did you smoke during a work break or a phone call, or because someone suggested a smoke? Perhaps you smoked each time you got in the car or before going to bed at night? As you look at your records from the last seven days, see whether a pattern starts to emerge. Perhaps you could use a number of different-coloured highlighter pens to highlight similar triggers, and identify a pattern that way?

Take as much time as you need and check every entry in your diary. Then, in the space provided, write down the smoking associations or triggers that you've identified. Identify your pattern briefly—for example 'with telephone calls', 'with coffee', 'when stressed'.

Smoking associations/triggers I've identified

_____

_____

_____

_____

_____

_____

_____

_____

_____

Beliefs about smoking

Once you have finished the list, I want you to ask yourself what beliefs you hold in connection with smoking. For instance, if you find that you always have a cigarette when you drink coffee, is this because you have a belief that 'Coffee tastes better with a cigarette'? Or, if you smoke when you're anxious, do you find yourself thinking, 'When I'm stressed a cigarette helps me relax'?

Take some time now to consider the beliefs you associate with smoking. You have probably realised by now that your belief, association, excuse or reason for smoking is a limiting belief.

List each of your limiting beliefs and how the thought makes you feel in the space below. I've included one example to get you started.

Limiting belief   **Emotion**
I can't stop smoking.   Helpless

_____

_____

_____

_____

_____

_____

_____

_____

_____

_____

Techniques for altering a limiting belief

We change our beliefs regularly. For example, when you were in high school you believed you were a high school student, then the day you left school that belief was no longer true so you changed it. The day you turned 18, you no longer had the belief that you were 17.

Our memories are stored in what can be described as a filing cabinet in the unconscious. Your unconscious mind stores and organises all your memories.

Following are three methods to help you transform and give new meaning to the old limiting beliefs. The first method will allow you to go back to the time when the belief started. The second method is aimed at forming new beliefs about yourself and using affirmations to reinforce these new beliefs. The third method is a self-hypnosis session that will allow you to disconnect from your past beliefs about smoking. If you follow each of the exercises to the best of your ability, they will destroy the old, limiting beliefs and set you free to form new, healthy beliefs.

Method 1: Finding your limiting belief

Many people carry around with them limiting beliefs that they believe, without question, to be the truth. But all limiting beliefs are preceded by a limiting decision—a decision to accept that belief. For example, the belief that coffee tastes better with cigarettes had to begin somewhere—the point at which you decided to adopt that belief.

When you go back to the root cause of this belief, you will be able to give new meaning to the belief and to the decision. By doing so, the belief will suddenly be transformed from something you accepted unquestioningly as true to something in which you no longer believe. When you give new meaning to the belief you once held, the old meaning disappears.

It is possible that the belief—in our example, the idea that coffee tastes better with cigarettes—started long before you even began smoking. It is possible the belief had started after or during your first cup of coffee with a cigarette. It is also possible there may have been other smokers in your family, or you may have seen something on TV or heard somebody make the statement that is now your belief.

You may have heard the evidence that unborn babies are affected in many ways by their parents' attitudes, actions and interactions. As bad as it is, I don't mean the effect of cigarette smoke on an unborn baby; rather, I'm talking about the influence of the emotional state, thoughts, actions and behaviour of those close to the baby.

You may even come from a long line of smokers, way back to your great-grandparents, and maybe they liked cigarettes with their coffee. If this is the case, then it is possible your limiting belief goes back down what is referred to as your genealogical (family) line. It is important to cover all possibilities because it's important to get to the root cause, the very beginning, of the belief.

You may say: 'I can't remember when it began. How would I know when it was?' Saying you can't remember is also a limiting belief. In fact, everything is recorded in your unconscious mind— everything. Trust your unconscious.

Once you've identified the origin of your limiting belief, you will be free to discover a 'positive learning'. Positive learnings are personal, so they are about you. They are also resources or new ways of thinking and beliefs for the future. Ideally, positive learnings are not negative; nor are they about others or about the past. For example, a learning such as 'Coffee tastes terrible with cigarettes and because I believed what other people believed I must have been pretty stupid' is not really an empowering positive learning. A positive learning is a learning that relates to you, and from which you are likely to benefit in the future. Your unconscious knows what you need to know to let go of the old belief—all you need to do is trust your unconscious. For example, if the limiting belief is that coffee tastes better with a cigarette, the positive learning could be: 'I enjoy coffee for the fresh taste of coffee.' If the limiting belief is 'I am a smoker', the positive learning could be 'I am happy breathing fresh air and lead a fulfilling crutch-free life.'

Before we discover the origins of your limiting beliefs, we will do an exercise to help you discover your own internal timeline, and thus where your memories are stored.

Read this through a few times before trying it so that you will know what to do.

Finding your timeline

We all have memories stored from the past—such as a friend from school, our first job, first bicycle, first car or a favourite holiday. Your memories are all stored in your past timeline. You also have future memories. You put events and memories into what is known as your future timeline. For example, you may have an event you are going to in a week or month from now. This memory, rather than being stored with past events, is stored in the future part of your time line. An appointment coming up with a doctor, a holiday you have planned, a future dinner party are all examples of future memories as opposed to memories from the past.

If you are ready, sit or lie down and make sure you are comfortable. Take a few deep breaths and relax. Then access the following memories:

First, recall an event from yesterday.

Next, go back further in time and recall a past holiday.

Now go back further and remember being in school. Recall a specific friend or teacher, and remember being in the classroom.

Go further back now and recall being a young child. Remember a happy time.

Now, imagine you are driving down the highway of your life, passing a stream of happy memories floating past the window.

Now come back up through the teenage years to the present. When you are back in the present, use one finger to point in the direction of your past—trust your unconscious mind and point. Your past could be in any direction—forward, back, left or right. Wherever you pointed is correct—however you store your memories is right for you. Take a mental note of where your timeline is.

What direction is your memory?

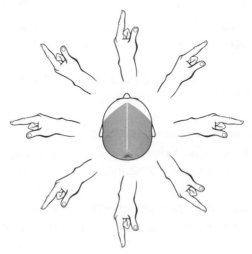

Next, imagine yourself in the future—it could be tomorrow, next month, a year away or next Christmas—whenever you want it to be.

Now, in your mind's eye, float all the way out to that future and, using the same finger as before, point in the direction of your future. Once again, this could be any direction. However you store your memories is just right. Take a mental note of the direction in which your future memories are stored. Now that you have discovered the direction of your timeline and been for a test drive, you will be ready to find past events and begin giving new meaning to the old beliefs.

Now you're going to use your timeline to identify the origin of your limiting belief and go back before it in order to let it go by asking your unconscious mind to give you a positive learning.

Your timeline

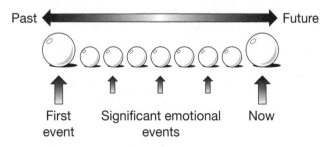

Discovering your positive learning

Step 1: Select your limiting belief (in our example, it is that coffee tastes better with a cigarette).

Step 2: Ask your unconscious what was the root cause of that limiting belief and when the limiting decision started.

Step 3: Write down the time of the root cause event. What age were you or at what time in your past did you make the decision?

Step 4: Imagine you are floating over and above this event and the decision to accept the belief.

Step 5: Now ask yourself what is the positive learning that will allow the old belief to disappear. Continue asking until you have a positive learning. All the answers are within you. Trust your unconscious to give you a positive learning that will allow the old belief to disappear. It may take anywhere from instantly to several minutes to get a positive learning. You may also choose to write down the positive learning in the space provided.

Step 6: Take the positive learning and float higher up and further back into the past before that event or any of the

events that led to it. From this position above and before the event, turn back and look towards the event and ask yourself, 'Where is the old belief now?' You may have noticed it has just disappeared.

Step 7: Float back to the present. Next, recall a specific time in the past when you may have had that old belief. Go back to that time and ask yourself: 'Where is that old belief now?' It should have disappeared.

Step 8: Imagine an unspecified time in the future which might previously have triggered the old limiting belief. Ask yourself: 'Where is the old belief now? What is there now?' You may discover with some delight that the old belief has been transformed into a new, empowering, positive belief.

Note: The only time a belief does not disappear is if you have not succeeded in recalling the very first event or you are not far enough back or high enough up above the event. You must also be in agreement with yourself about letting go of the old belief.

Method 2: New belief affirmations

Where there be negative thinking let there be reflection to the contrary.
—Patanjali, *The Yoga Sutras*, second century BC

An affirmation is a declaration of sorts. This is more of a conscious exercise, and you may even use many of your learnings from the previous method with your timeline. The positive thought will still likely come from your unconscious, but the idea of an affirmation is that you repeat it over and over like a mantra.

With this exercise, you will first write down a series of limiting beliefs and then come up with your own empowering beliefs that contradict them. List the limiting beliefs on the left-hand side. Then physically cross out the limiting belief and write down the positive belief on the right-hand side of the page. Here are a few examples:

Limiting belief	Positive belief
~~I am a smoker~~	I am happy and smoke-free
~~I can't stop smoking~~	I easily stop smoking
~~I can't handle the cravings~~	I crush the cravings with enthusiasm
~~It's too hard~~	I make it easy

Now write down your own positive beliefs alongside these common limiting beliefs.

Limiting belief	Positive belief
I am a smoker.	_____
I can't stop smoking.	_____
I can't handle the cravings.	_____
It's too hard.	_____
Cigarettes are my friend.	
Coffee tastes better with a cigarette.	_____
Having a smoke relaxes me.	_____
I enjoy a cigarette with a drink.	_____
I enjoy watching TV with a cigarette.	_____
A meal is not complete without a cigarette.	_____
I have to smoke while driving.	_____
I like a cigarette while on the phone.	_____

I'll never be able to stop. _____

A cigarette is a great chance
  to chat with friends. _____

Smoking is social. _____

List any other limiting beliefs you may have then cross them
out and write the new empowering belief.

_____

_____

_____

_____

Method 3: Self-hypnosis for disconnecting past connections

Congratulations on making the choice to be *smoke-free*, to be a *non-smoker*. You know you have made the right choice.

The following self-hypnosis session is to be read in the evening after you have had your last cigarette and before going to sleep. You may like to play some calming instrumental music while reading through the following session. This session is one of your bonus MP3 downloads. Take on board all the suggestions that are right for you, and allow the positive suggestions to embed themselves in the deepest part of your unconscious.

I will be asking you to make some pictures in your mind. As you know, some people make pictures easily, some feel things more intensely, and others may hear things inside their head and hear the voices of others, so whatever works for you is OK. Maybe you will get a feeling, maybe an idea or an image.

Sit down and find a comfortable upright position. Let go of any worries and tensions, let any problems drift away. If any music is playing, take a few moments to listen to it, breathing deeply in and out; double your relaxation with every out breath.

Imagine you are standing at the top of a flight of ten steps. As you go down each of the ten steps, you will become more deeply relaxed. Count down from ten to one, becoming more relaxed with each step. Count backwards from ten now. When you descend the last step, you find you are in a room. An old-fashioned switchboard is on the opposite wall with plugs and black cords everywhere and an old-fashioned seat in front of it. Make your way over to the switchboard and sit down on the seat. As you sit there looking at all the black cords and plugs, your desire for success sweeps over you. You realise you are willing to do whatever it takes to achieve your goal.

At the top of the switchboard, you see a sign that reads: A SMOKE-FREE LIFE. And you know this is what you desire deep within you—a smoke-free life.

Then you realise that you are in the control room of your unconscious mind, the part deep within you that heals your body, controls your thoughts and knows exactly what you want, deep inside.

The more you think about what you desire, the more you realise it is time to lead a smoke-free life. You want this more than anything, you are hungry for it. You have to be hungry to achieve your goal. You are ready to live a smoke-free life.

As you look at all the black cords and plugs, you notice that above each one is a little sign. Each of these signs begins with the word smoking. The first one you look at reads: *Smoking the first cigarette of the day.* Now you realise that, because you are a non-smoker, you need to disconnect that plug.

You reach up and take hold of the black rubber cord. You pull the plug out at one end, disconnecting it, and then you pull it out at the other end. You hold the unplugged cord in your hand for a moment, then throw it into the rubbish bin beside you. In your mind you hear yourself say: 'I will never have that first cigarette of the day again', and you feel a sense of relief. You also realise that if there is no first cigarette of the day, you are now smoke-free.

The next sign reads: *Smoking when drinking coffee.* Take this cord and pull it out, unplugging it at both ends. You don't need this connection anymore because you just stopped smoking. You are completely smoke-free. You now lead *a smoke-free life.* You throw the cord in the bin with the other one, and you notice how good it feels to never smoke again while drinking coffee. You quietly repeat in your mind: 'Coffee tastes great just as it is.'

The next sign reads: *Smoking after finishing a meal.* You take the cord and pull it out at both ends because you just stopped smoking: you are completely smoke-free. You now lead *a smoke-free life.* You throw this cord in the bin too, and you notice how good it feels to never smoke again after a meal. You know the smell and taste of the food is so much better as a non-smoker. You just stopped smoking and you have no desire to ever touch another cigarette because you are a non-smoker. You quietly repeat in your mind: 'I enjoy finishing a meal and savouring the taste of the meal in a natural and healthy way.'

As you look back at the switchboard, you notice another sign which reads: *Smoking while driving.* You take that cord and you disconnect it, pulling the cord out at both ends and throwing it in the bin. You have no need to ever smoke again in a car because you are now smoke-free, you are now a non-smoker, and you are happy that you are now smoke-free. You quietly repeat in your mind: 'I drive my car as a happy non-smoker.'

The next sign reads: *Smoking during breaks.* You disconnect this one too. You pull out both plugs and you throw the cord in the bin. You will never have a cigarette break again. You have no desire to have a cigarette break because you are now smoke-free.

You think about all the things you can do instead of smoking: you can practise deep-breathing exercises or sip cold, fresh water. You can do an exercise or activity that makes you feel good, or you can sit calmly and take the time to relax because you are now smoke-free. You have simply stopped smoking. You repeat in your mind: 'I enjoy breathing fresh air and eating nutritious foods or drinking healthy teas during my break.'

The next sign on the switchboard reads: *Smoking when socialising.* You realise it is easy to socialise and be a non-smoker, so you reach up and pull out the black cord at both ends and throw it in the bin. You have no need, no desire to ever smoke again. You have just stopped! You are now smoke-free, completely and totally smoke-free. You repeat in your mind: 'I now socialise in a healthy, happy way.'

The next sign reads: *Smoking when bored.* You reach up and disconnect this cord at both ends and throw it in the bin. That connection is now gone forever. You no longer know the meaning of the word 'bored'. You have too much to live for. You have so many choices: to be active, to take up hobbies, to try out things that you have wanted to do for a long time. You have new choices now, because you are smoke-free, you are now a non-smoker. You feel confident and strong in the fact you are a non-smoker. You will never desire another cigarette again, because you are smoke-free. You repeat in your mind: 'My life is exciting and fulfilling.'

As you look over the switchboard you notice that there are a number of other connections. These represent connections you formed in the past by choosing to smoke at particular times and for particular reasons, such as when you felt stressed, worried, anxious or angry. Look over the switchboard now and pull out every connection that you can see. With each cord that you pull out and throw into the bin, consider each connection you are undoing.

Ask yourself now whether there are events that would make you want a cigarette. If any connections or associations remain, pull them out now, rip them all out and throw them in the bin. You have no need to ever smoke again, because you just stopped. You are now smoke-free. You are a non-smoker. Repeat in your mind or aloud three times:

I am now smoke-free. I am now a non-smoker.
I am now smoke-free. I am now a non-smoker.
I am now smoke-free. I am now a non-smoker.

Whenever you feel stressed, you now have so many ways to relax and unwind.

As each day passes, your strength grows, your confidence grows. You hear yourself in your mind, repeating the phrase:

The new me is smoke-free. The new me is smoke-free. The new me is smoke-free.

It is time now to leave that old switchboard behind. But before you go, you look behind the switchboard and notice the main power cord going into the wall and you pull it out. You have now totally disconnected and turned off the old switchboard that used to control you. The connections are no longer there so you have no need to ever smoke again. You have no desire to ever smoke again, because you are now smoke-free. You are now a happy non-smoker.

As you turn around and walk away from that old switchboard and your past as a smoker, you notice the room has become brighter. Looking around the room, you now see pictures on the walls. You walk over to look at them and you realise they are photos of you—the new you, active, free and healthy. In some pictures, family and friends are smiling with you—they are happy that you have given away that disgusting habit, happy that you are now smoke-free. There is one photo of you with your doctor and the doctor is smiling, he is giving you two thumbs up, because you have just had a check-up and your health is improving rapidly.

YOUR CIRCULATION IMPROVES.

YOUR LUNG FUNCTION INCREASES.

YOUR SENSE OF SMELL COMPLETELY RETURNS.

YOU FEEL GREAT.

There are more pictures of you enjoying your life and being healthy. Then you notice another sign that says:

YOU ARE COMPLETELY HEALTHY.

You realise that your body has *a blueprint for perfect health*. You realise you have had your last cigarette and you will never touch another cigarette again. Your body begins to heal itself immediately and you are happy to be smoke-free.

You stand in the middle of the room taking in everything around you, all the important messages about health, financial and social benefits. You begin to think about all the things you can do to be healthier. Your health is now your number one priority, and you know that now you are a non-smoker your health will improve every day. You will never pick up or touch another cigarette again. Quietly repeat in your mind:

THE NEW ME IS SMOKE-FREE.
THE NEW ME IS SMOKE-FREE.
THE NEW ME IS SMOKE-FREE.

Congratulations, you have had your last cigarette and you will never touch another cigarette again. You are now *happy to be smoke-free.*

What is the most important thing in your life right now? Is it your family? Is it your career? If you said your health is the most important thing in your life, congratulations. In a minute you will reinforce that understanding. If you believe another area of your life is more important than your health, think about that for a moment: without your health you would have less energy and not be well enough for all the other important aspects of life. Isn't it at least equal top priority? You now realise that to be healthy you need to eat balanced, healthy meals. You need to drink more water. You need to avoid sugary or caffeinated drinks and refined starchy foods. You need to have adequate physical activity.

Your health will improve day by day as your body heals and you become stronger, because you are now a non-smoker. Health and well-being are now your priority. Count up from one to ten.

YOU ARE NOW A NON-SMOKER.

YOU ARE NOW SMOKE-FREE.

THE NEW ME IS SMOKE-FREE.

THE NEW ME IS SMOKE-FREE.

THE NEW ME IS SMOKE-FREE.

Q-DAY: SMOKE-FREE FOREVER

The Think Quit Mantra

The new me is smoke-free.
I am a happy non-smoker.

It is my choice to be smoke-free.
I now choose health over cigarettes.

I now choose happiness in my life.
For as long as I live, I will never touch another cigarette.

The new me is Smoke-Free
Forever.

Welcome to the first day of the rest of your life. In fact, every day from now on will be the first day of the rest of your life—a life free from smoking. You are now a non-smoker. You are free from smoke.

Repeat: I am now ready. Today is the day to be smoke-free. I am now a non-smoker.

For a long time now, you have wanted to quit smoking and you have finally done it—you have just stopped and you are now smoke-free. For many years of your life, you did in fact live nicotine-free—for the first 12, 15 or 20 years of your life you probably never touched a cigarette. Remember this feeling, as you change your life, as you become smoke-free.

After following the Seven-Day Preparation Program, you now know how to breathe properly, how to relax and how to easily overcome any cravings that may attempt to sneak in. You can now go ahead with your life with the knowledge that *your mind has changed*.

Acupressure points to help you stay smoke-free

Acupuncture has been used for thousands of years in Chinese traditional medicine and has helped people overcome back problems, internal organ illness and a wide range of other health disorders. Today, many people use acupuncture as a complementary support to Western orthodox medicine. As you will not be sticking acupuncture needles into yourself, you will learn several points to massage using acupressure, which is like acupuncture except you will be using your thumbs or fingers to massage the energy points.

Headache points

The first point we will cover helps with headaches, which are sometimes a side-effect when stopping smoking. The headache points are also good for energising the mind.

Instruction: When performing acupressure, massage each point on both the left and right sides of your body three times for approximately 10 to 20 seconds. You can massage in a linear (small straight line) or circular motion.

Headache point on the hand

The main headache point on the hand is found by making your hand flat with your thumb and fingers locked together. The highest point of the muscle next to the base of your thumb is the acupressure point. Put the thumb of your free hand on the point. Relax the hand that you are going to massage and begin rubbing the point. Massage this point on the back of both hands thoroughly. Massage for between 10 and 20 seconds. Repeat three times on both hands.

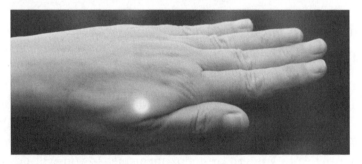

Eyebrow point

The eyebrow point is great for relieving headaches. It is found two finger widths out from the bridge of your nose and on the underside of your eyebrow arch. Massage this point on both sides with the thumb three times for 10 to 20 seconds each time.

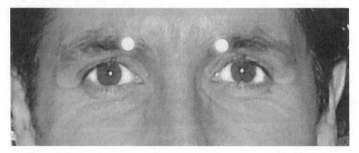

Temples

Start near the corner of the eyes and, with three fingers together, massage in small circles over the temple and into the hairline. You can massage by applying direct pressure, by rubbing back and forth or by rubbing in a circular motion. Repeat three times for 10 to 20 seconds each time on both sides.

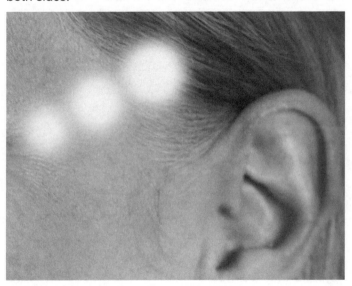

To strengthen lungs

Lung point on thumb

Massage the point at the corner of the base of your nail on the outside of your thumb. Put the thumb of your free hand on the point and rub in a small circular or linear motion for between 10 and 20 seconds. Repeat this three times on both hands. This point is particularly good for a sore throat and asthma. (See image on page 200.)

Lung point on hand

This point helps relieve coughs and a sore throat. Massage the point on the palm of the hand at the centre of the fleshy mound near the base of the thumb. Massage using the thumb of your other hand three times for 10 to 20 seconds. The point may feel sore. Gently massage, and breathe slowly and deeply while massaging until the pain subsides.

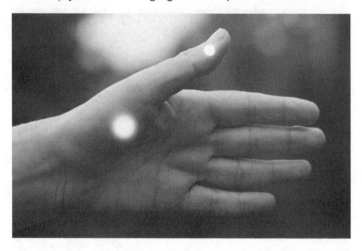

Stop-smoking points

Stop-smoking acupressure points on the wrist

There are three points to massage. The point in the centre is the main stop-smoking acupressure point. Massaging these points on both wrists can help reduce cravings and change the taste or desire you have for cigarettes. The extra points either side of the stop-smoking point are also good for headache and sore throat. The points are located in the concave depression between the tendons at the crease area of your wrist, as seen in the photo on page 201. When stretching your thumb back, it is easier to find the points. Massage these points using moderate pressure with your thumb from your other hand three times for a period of 10 to 20 seconds.

Stop-smoking points on the ear

This point on the ear is known in Chinese as the *shenmen* point, which translates to mean 'heavenly gate'. Massaging this point allows you to feel calm and grounded, and it is a popular point in laser therapy, acupuncture and acupressure. This point helps relax the mind and body, reduces stress, is beneficial for anxiety as well as insomnia, and can be used to reduce pain and stop cravings related to addictions.

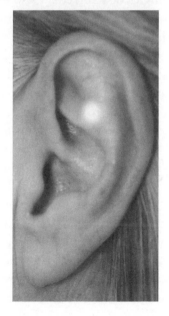

Massage each ear point three times for 10 to 20 seconds. Massage by placing the thumb over the point on the inside of the ear and the index finger behind the ear. You can pinch the point with your index finger and thumb or massage around in a small circle between your thumb and finger.

Q-Day self-hypnosis sessions

The following hypnosis sessions encapsulate much of what you have learnt over the past week in preparation to lead a smoke-free life. These sessions will add force to your resolve to be vigilant in your desire to remain smoke-free forever. You will never touch another cigarette again as you work through these two sessions today. Read 'The Secret Library' at the beginning of the day and 'Smoke-Free Forever' after a short break or in the evening before going to bed. You could also repeat these sessions as often as you like. For some people, reading through once will be enough, while others may need to go through them every day for 21 days or longer. These two sessions are the main stop-smoking sessions in the Think Quit program, and are also available as part of the MP4 program found in the resource section at the back of the book.

Remember you get a Q-Day stop-smoking session as a download. Make sure you listen to this session.

Self-hypnosis: The Secret Library

Sit or lie down and make yourself really comfortable. Then relax, focusing on your breathing and picture the following as you read. If you like, you can listen to a piece of music in the background.

The phrase you are going to repeat over and over in your mind is: *The new me is smoke-free.* Inhale now and say in your mind the words *The new me*, then exhale, saying *is smoke-free.* With every outward breath, double your levels of relaxation. Slowly and deeply breathe in and out, your body relaxing and your muscles becoming softer and looser. When you are ready, begin the self-hypnosis session.

Imagine in your mind's eye that you are about to enter a secret library. The answers to everything you need to know are behind the door in front of you. The door is heavy and you have to use both arms to push it open. Inside the room, the walls are lined with bookshelves full of books. The rows of books cover the walls all the way up to the ceiling.

In the middle of the room is a large dark brown leather chair. You walk towards it and see that an envelope has been left on the chair. On the envelope is written the instruction: 'Sit down and open the envelope and read the message.' Inside the envelope is a folded piece of paper. You unfold the paper and read: 'To the non-smoker, congratulations.'

You sit down on the chair. It is very comfortable, and you relax and close your eyes for a few moments and consider the reasons why you have made the choice to be a non-smoker. Having pondered some of the main reasons why you are now smoke-free, you continue reading.

The note continues: 'From this day forward you are smoke-free. You are now a non-smoker with no desire to smoke—you don't like smoke and because you don't like smoke you will never smoke again. Smoking for you is now in the past: it was something you did for one period of your life, it was a stage you went through, but now you are smoke-free. You are proud to be a non-smoker and proud to be smoke-free.'

While you sit in the chair, consider your life as a non-smoker. Think of some of the things you will do as a non-smoker, think about how clean your hair will smell, how fresh your breath will be—no more smelly clothes, no more coughing, no more shortness of breath, and no more worrying that the smoke, the poisons and the nicotine will make you sick.

Next, you read that you have a task. Your task is to find a book or books on the shelves that will help you be smoke-free.

You make your way up and down the aisles glancing at the book titles. You notice a beautiful burgundy-coloured, leather-bound book. The book's title immediately captivates you: *My Life as a Non-smoker*. You take the book from the shelf and sit back down in the comfortable chair.

Opening the book, you flick through its pages. The book is set in the old cursive style and you find it easy to read. As you read, you realise that many people have gone down the path that lies ahead of you and that you are not alone, you are not the first and you will not be the last.

The heading on one page reads: 'Nothing Can Throw You'. Below this heading you read: 'You are now strong and in control; you have no desire to touch another cigarette again. You will be as mentally, physically and spiritually strong as anyone else who has ever travelled this path. You will be in total control of your life.' You let this thought seal itself in the deepest part of your unconscious.

Nothing can throw me.

I am mentally, physically and spiritually strong.

I am in total control of my life.

The next page is headed: 'You Have No Interest in Smoking'. Underneath the heading, the text continues: 'You no longer desire cigarettes, you no longer desire to smoke, you only desire things in life that are healthy and good for you. You choose health over poison from this day forward. You have no interest in smoking and you won't even give it another thought, because you are now a non-smoker, you are now smoke-free.' Again, you let the thoughts seal themselves in the deepest part of your unconscious.

I no longer desire cigarettes.

I only desire things in life that are good for me.

I now choose health.

I am now a non-smoker.

I am now smoke-free.

The feelings of being smoke-free flow through you as you reinforce the positive new thoughts that will now be a major part of your life.

You read another page of the book. Here the heading is: 'You Have Overcome'. This section reads: 'The need for smoking is gone and you feel relieved that you no longer need to smoke. You feel happy that you are now a non-smoker. You finally feel free from the clutches of the old life-sapping habit. Never again will you poison your body in any way, shape or form. You now think of making your body healthy, and treating your self with love and respect because this is the vehicle that will carry you around for the rest of your life. The need for smoking is gone.'

I am a happy non-smoker.

I am finally free.

I now make my body healthy.

I treat myself with love and respect.

You go back to the book and read on. 'You have an inner strength, and each and every time you replace the old habit with a new habit you will build that strength. The strength within you will increase every day. Each day becomes easier and easier as you totally forget about cigarettes. This gives you the increased confidence and self-esteem of a winner.'

I am strong.

I have high self-esteem.

I am a self-confident winner.

You know that you are now smoke-free. The fact you have done this means you can do many other things. You feel very happy with yourself, knowing that you have done the right thing for yourself. From this moment on, you are stronger than ever before, you are more determined, more focused. Your determination increases with every passing minute of every passing day. With each passing day this strength is growing within you. You are easily able to overcome all obstacles and challenges.

I am now smoke-free.

I am happy and have done the right thing.

I am determined and focused.

I easily overcome all obstacles and challenges.

The next page of the book you are reading says: 'You are in Control'. It continues: 'You realise that you have the choice not to smoke because you have so many other things you choose to do instead. If you get any of the old feelings you know you can take ten slow deep breaths, run on the spot, sip some water, eat a quarter of an orange or apple, or do ten push-ups. You now choose to be healthy and active. You realise smoking serves no useful purpose and you have so many alternatives.'

I am an in-control person.

I choose to be smoke-free.

I choose to be healthy and active.

The next page of the first book is headed: 'The Happy Choice'. It goes on: 'You now realise that smoking is unhealthy and it has brought you much unhappiness and stress. Now that you have so many choices, you are happy you have no need to ever smoke again. You are now smoke-free, you are now a happy non-smoker.'

I am now smoke-free.

I am a happy non-smoker.

The heading on the next page reads: 'Thoughts of a Cigarette Disgust You'. It tells you how the thought of tobacco makes you feel ill, and you realise as you watch other people smoking how crazy it is. How could they put that vile substance into their bodies? The smell of tobacco on others is now magnified. As your sense of smell returns, you realise how awful the smell of tobacco and smoke is on their clothes, in their hair, on their breath, and you feel good because you are now smoke-free. You can say to yourself:

The new me is smoke-free.

The new me is smoke-free.

The new me is smoke-free.

The heading on the next page of the book is: 'No Thoughts of Cigarettes'. 'From now on, as you focus on breathing clean air and improving your health, you will only focus on what you want. From this moment forward, you only allow clean, fresh air to enter your lungs. You don't have any need or desire to ever smoke again. You have no thoughts of smoking. You and you alone are in control. You can change your thoughts *in an instant*. You easily redirect your thinking to healthy choices. Smoking no longer exists in your life, in your world. Smoking is now gone. Gone forever.'

I only allow clean air to enter my lungs.

I change my thoughts in an instant.

I direct my thinking to healthy choices.

You finish reading the book and decide to put it away with the others. As you pick it up to place it on the shelf, you realise the quote on the back is your saying: 'The new me is smoke-free. The new me is smoke-free. The new me is smoke-free.' You realise this is all you need to think at any time, day or night, on your own or with a group. This is the saying that dictates your life from now on, and you quietly think: 'The new me is smoke-free. The new me is smoke-free. The new me is smoke-free.'

From this moment forward, you think of yourself not as an ex-smoker but as a non-smoker. Non-smokers have no need to even think about smoking, let alone have a cigarette.

You take all those lessons with you—everything you have learnt, everything you understand, is being sealed deep within your unconscious as you know your life as a non-smoker is a reality. It is a good life, a healthier life, a happier life, because you are smoke-free.

When you are ready, you leave the library but you know that you can return there at any time to strengthen your resolve to remain smoke-free.

Focus on your breathing as you bring feeling back into your arms and legs. Stretch and wriggle your fingers and toes. Move your arms and legs and return your awareness to your body. As you breathe more deeply, know the only thing you need to remember is: *The new me is smoke-free. The new me is smoke-free. The new me is smoke-free.*

Stretch your arms above your head. Bringing them down again, you draw energy into your body, you draw enthusiasm, confidence, self-esteem and control, because you now have the skills and tools necessary to take control of your life, to be a non-smoker, to be smoke-free.

Now slowly open your eyes, then take a few moments to gather your energy and thoughts. Maybe you stretch and breathe more deeply, be more focused, be more determined ... for now you are smoke-free; you are now a non-smoker; you are smoke-free forever.

Enjoy the good feelings associated with being smoke-free.

Self-hypnosis: Smoke-free forever

The following self-hypnosis session is a second session you could go through to reinforce the fact you are now smoke-free. You might like to take a break and come back to it later during the day or this evening before going to bed.

Sit down and get comfortable as you read this session to yourself quietly in your mind or have somebody else read it to you. As you read every word, feel your eyes move across the page. With each blink, relax more deeply. Feel your breathing flowing in and out as you relax your shoulders.

Hear the noises around you, but more importantly hear your own voice inside as you carefully read every single word to yourself. As you read, you realise nothing is more important than your health. Health is what you value most in your life.

Repeat three times quietly to yourself or out loud:

> Health is my number one priority.
> Health is my number one priority.
> Health is my number one priority.

As you think about cigarettes and the damage they are doing and have done to your body, you begin to hate them, you begin to loathe and despise cigarettes. They are the most vile things on the planet.

Compare cigarettes to the most disgusting substance you can imagine. It could be burning rubber. It could be cleanings from your toenails.

Smoking is not cool, it is not fun nor is it relaxing. Smoking is toxic and it disgusts you. Cigarettes are nothing more than toxic poison rolled up in a tiny piece of paper, and you would be crazy to ever touch one. You will never touch another cigarette again, and after making that choice you will float off out into the future. Float out over the years all the way out to a brighter, happier, healthier future.

Float all the way to the very end of your future timeline and stop just before it, on the verandah of your life. Imagine you are sitting there and you are quite old, maybe in your eighties, maybe even in your nineties, but you are older and wiser and you are healthy. You are well, because you have made health your top priority. You hear the thought in your mind: *Nothing is more important than my health. Health is my number one priority.*

As you sit there, you look back over all the years, over all the joy and happiness you have had as a non-smoker, how life was good, is good and always will be good as a non-smoker. And from this future point you look back over the years to this moment, your Q-Day, the day you became smoke-free, the day from which you never touched another cigarette again, because you are a non-smoker, you have no need to touch another cigarette again, and you are happy with the choice you made. From that vantage point, you realise cigarettes were never a friend! That was just an illusion. You realise you were never half as addicted as you thought you were, that it was quite easy for you to become smoke-free.

Go ahead now and float all the way back over the healthy years, over the smoke-free years of your life, and notice yourself doing everything easily and effortlessly, all those joys in life, a smoke-free life. You are living a happy, healthy life because you changed your way of thinking, making health your number one priority. Again you hear the thought in your mind: *Nothing is more important than my health. Health is my number one priority.*

Floating back to now, I want you to imagine just for a moment that you are smoking a cigarette. As you put the cigarette to your lips, in your mind's eye, it is like burning rubber or tar, the vilest substance you can imagine: that rubber or tar is burning through your mouth, down into your lungs, and burning away parts of your insides. Imagine rubber dripping down your throat—the cigarette feels like it is burning you. The cigarette feels like it is killing you, poisoning you, and the poison drips down into your body and you feel as if your lungs are burning away, and the smell of smoke going into your nose burns your nostrils. You cannot stand the smell and taste of cigarettes, they become the most repulsive, the most disgusting substance on the planet—nothing is more disgusting than a cigarette. If a cigarette were to ever touch your lips again it would instantly make you feel ill and you would throw it away. You hear yourself repeating in your mind or out loud:

I cannot stand the taste of cigarettes.

Cigarettes are repulsive and disgust me.

Nothing is more disgusting than a cigarette.

I will never touch another cigarette again.

I have made the choice to be smoke-free, to be a non-smoker, to have health and joy and happiness in my life, and I do not need cigarettes to do that.

Now imagine yourself floating out again into the future—a day or a week into the future—and you see other people smoking and you wonder how you ever did it. You know what they are doing to themselves; you know that they are poisoning themselves, a little bit at a time; you now know they are killing themselves and you no longer ignore that fact. You look at your friends, or even strangers, and as they smoke you feel sorry for them. You realise their thinking is clouded by the cigarette smoke, clouded by their old patterns, their old associations, and you are so happy now because you have so many options to replace the old habit, you have no need to ever touch another cigarette again. Imagine someone is offering you a cigarette, and you easily and effortlessly say to yourself: *The new me is smoke-free. I am now a non-smoker.* Then you politely say, 'No thank you, I don't smoke.' You may even choose to tell them how you did it so easily and effortlessly.

You have no desire to ever touch another cigarette again—maybe even the smell of a cigarette begins to disgust you. You do not want to be near cigarette smoke because it makes you sick. You are repulsed by the thought or the smell of cigarettes to the point where you almost want to vomit and have to leave the area, your stomach churning with a nauseated feeling whenever you smell cigarettes. You do not even want to be near cigarette smoke. You'll never, ever smoke again. If you ever have a thought of smoking you repeat in your mind:

THE NEW ME IS SMOKE-FREE.

Smokers are chokers, and you are no longer a choker. You're a happy non-smoker. You believe it now, because you are a non-smoker. You will never smoke again. You will never crave another cigarette again. You will never think about smoking again. Smoking is erased from your memory.

Now look within yourself, into your memory, and find the unconscious part of your mind, that part of your mind where you had recorded the thought of being a smoker. Imagine you are now inside that part of your brain, and it is like a big blackboard with notes written over it in chalk—notes like 'Coffee tastes better with a cigarette', 'I like to smoke in the car', 'After a meal', 'With friends', and so on. Now imagine you take a big blackboard duster and you are wiping away those old messages, those old thoughts until the blackboard is completely blank, because you now have no desire for cigarettes.

Imagine now you are writing with chalk on the blackboard:

The new me is smoke-free.

I am now a non-smoker.

Nothing is more important than my health.

You may like to imagine yourself writing these phrases three or four times on the board as you repeat them over and over.

The new me is smoke-free.

I am now a non-smoker.

Nothing is more important than my health.

This saying—*The new me is smoke-free; I am now a non-smoker; Nothing is more important than my health*—now becomes your mantra. You repeat it as often as needed until you just forget to smoke.

You can forget so easily, and with forgetting certain things you can remember other things. You remember what you need to remember and forget what you want to forget. It's easy to forget. Who cares what you ate for lunch on a rainy Wednesday two weeks ago? You just forget all about it. Maybe you forget to smoke. You forget things easily and effortlessly. Your unconscious remembers everything that you need to remember and you can let your unconscious remember while your conscious mind sleeps and forgets.

Magically and suddenly, you are smoke-free, with no need to touch another cigarette again. In the blink of an eye, you have changed your mind. You easily choose to be smoke-free. You are now a non-smoker. Non-smokers do not touch cigarettes. Non-smokers do not even think of smoking cigarettes. You just forget to smoke. You are now a non-smoker.

Cast away any thought of smoking. It does not interest you. You are happy to be free. You have broken free from the nicotine prison. You are now free. You are now a non-smoker.

You are aware of your breathing and your body. You think of all the things you can do, how healthy you can be, the activities you can undertake, even if that's just walking for ten, 15 or 20 minutes a day. You remember your breathing exercises, you remember to drink more water and eat healthy balanced meals every day. You are becoming happier, you are more energetic and enthusiastic, you are happy now because you have made the decision to never touch another cigarette again, and you know that each day your health will improve. In a few short years, your body and health will be back to that of a non-smoker. Your body has a blueprint for perfect health, and when you allow it to heal itself it will heal; when you give your body the environment to be healthy, it will be healthy. You look forward to your sense of smell returning, you enjoy being able to smell food and flowers and other everyday things. You also enjoy your sense of taste returning. You are in total control of your life.

Congratulations!

Busting those cravings

If you experience any cravings, you now have plenty of replacement strategies you can put in place.

You may also like to read the following craving-busting sessions. Refer back to them any time the need arises.

Think Quit craving-busting session 1

If you feel like you want a cigarette now—STOP! You are now a non-smoker, you are now smoke-free. Get excited because the nicotine is leaving your system. Quickly repeat in your mind three times:

> THE NEW ME IS SMOKE-FREE.
> THE NEW ME IS SMOKE-FREE.
> THE NEW ME IS SMOKE-FREE.

Immediately choose from the following list and go for it:

- Take ten deep breaths, in for ten out for ten.
- Take ten sips of water.
- Eat a quarter of an orange.
- Eat half an apple.
- Do ten push-ups.
- Power-walk across the room and count to ten, ten times.

You are now a non-smoker. You are now smoke-free. You do not smoke.

Think Quit craving-busting session 2

Repeat in your mind: *I am now a non-smoker. I am now smoke-free. I am a happy non-smoker.* If you are feeling stressed, practise one of the relaxation techniques or do a deep-breathing exercise. Here's a quick list for reference:

- Drink a glass of water.
- Breathe in for four, hold for two, out for four, hold for two.
- Breathe in for ten, out for ten.
- Breathe in THE NEW ME, breathe out IS SMOKE FREE.
- Practise Serenity.
- Practise the Tortoise pose.
- Work your acupressure points.

You could even practise Serenity or the Tortoise pose in your mind—imagine you are doing one of them now.

The key to your success is to replace the old habits with healthy new, life-giving habits. You might like to run on the spot for 30 seconds or a minute, or have a stretch—whatever it is, make your choice and start your new habits today.

Reinforce the new positive habits and repeat in your mind again:

> The new me is smoke-free.
> The new me is smoke-free.
> The new me is smoke-free.

Jenny's story

And whatever happened to Jenny? Remember our high-profile friend who had tried everything to give up. Step by step, Jenny followed the exercises found in this book. Jenny practised the breathing exercises and chi kung. She drank lots of water, started eating nutritious meals and began exercising regularly. In fact, to celebrate her first year as a non-smoker, Jenny went mountain climbing in Nepal. A year later, Jenny walked the Kokoda Trail! Rather than putting on weight, Jenny has maintained her weight while dramatically increasing her fitness. These days, Jenny is free from all the worries and associated problems that had weighed her down when smoking. The nagging colds and the cough are gone, as has the fear of falling ill with some hideous sickness. Jenny is now free, and said the key to her being free was her mindset of never needing a cigarette no matter what, the fact that she thinks of herself as a non-smoker and will never touch a cigarette as long as she lives. Jenny has made health the most important thing in her life and is reaping the rewards.

Wise advice

What advice would you give to a young person—somebody the same age you were when you started smoking—if they were about to light up their first cigarette but asked you, having been a long-term smoker, for some advice and why they should or shouldn't light up?

Write your answer to them in the space provided.

_____

_____

_____

_____

_____

_____

Imagine now that you have travelled back in time to the exact time and place of you about to light up that first cigarette. In your mind's eye, see, hear and feel yourself standing in front of the younger you and telling the younger you why you should not smoke. In light of your knowledge of the dangers, your years of experience and your wisdom, share this understanding. Be as descriptive and strong as you need to be while remaining thoughtful and having empathy.

Imagine now that you float back into the past before that first cigarette or before any of the chain of events that ever led to that first cigarette. In light of all that you now know, from that position way before that first cigarette, ask yourself where is the thought now of being a smoker. You may notice with some delight that it is gone. What do you believe about yourself now? If there is any trace of desire left, you may need to repeat this exercise on events such as watching role models smoke or any other earlier memory where you had thought of smoking.

It is time to totally forget to smoke.

Not one single puff, never ever

If you think you can have just one puff of a cigarette, this is a recipe for disaster. You may find stopping with Think Quit is easy—so easy, in fact, that you could be lulled in to a false sense of security that you could have just one, seeing as how you now have control. Don't kid yourself. Be vigilant, because the next time it may not be as easy. You need to be on guard as the sleeper effect can last for several years. You could go a month or longer and feel fantastic. Maybe even a year may pass and you are smoke-free. Then, for some unknown reason, the urge to have a cigarette pops up out of the blue. It generally passes quickly but some people fall into the trap. You may even kid yourself that you will just have one socially here and there, but you know what will happen. One will lead to two and so it will continue until you are back to the old habit or, even worse, you could end up smoking more. There is no good reason to ever smoke again. Divorce, death or getting the sack are not good reasons to start poisoning yourself again. As soon as you light up, you are back on the merry-go-round, only you won't be merry for very long when you realise you are hooked again. There is no reason to start smoking again at all, ever. You are much stronger than the addiction. Once you have broken the back of the addiction, there is no good reason to start again. Never, ever touch a cigarette again.

One puff and you will be back where you started.

Life as a non-smoker

Congratulations on working your way through the seven days and now being a non-smoker. This is the best thing you will ever do for your life and health. You will not miss anything. In fact, there will be another thousand things you can do now that you are smoke-free. You deserve to be smoke-free. You are worth it. You will never look back. It is time to totally forget to smoke.

You are now a non-smoker you are now smoke-free forever. This is the beginning of the story, your story!

Solutions to possible side-effects

Note: The following suggestions are not intended to replace the advice of a doctor or trained medical professional. Check with your doctor if any of the following symptoms persist.

As mentioned at the start of the book, some people in the days or weeks after stopping smoking may or may not have a few of the following symptoms. Your body needs to get back to normality. By practising the exercises and tips found in this book, you will go a long way towards either eliminating or reducing possible quit symptoms. In the same way a regular cold passes, so will any symptoms. You may be lucky and have none at all. The following tips are natural home remedies that you may choose to use if the need arises.

Anxiety

Anxiety is a warning to focus on what you want rather than what you don't want. Take a deep breath, relax and visualise a positive outcome rather than focusing on what is making you feel the anxiety.

Constipation

Constipation is often the result of not enough fluids, not enough fibre in your diet, not chewing well and irregular eating patterns. A long walk after dinner can help get the system moving. Prunes, dates and mangoes are known to help. A tablespoon of castor oil chased by a small cup of strong black coffee works a treat. Stay close to the bathroom. Carrot, beetroot, spinach and apple juice is a great drink and can relieve constipation. A tablespoon of linseed (flaxseed) oil over a salad or on your porridge can lubricate where needed. Freshly squeezed orange juice has been known to work wonders. Rolled oats for breakfast with bran or fruit salad can also help.

Coughing

Take extra vitamin C. Lozenges are OK in the short term to help overcome a scratchy throat or cough. Take extra garlic and horseradish tablets. Warm water with diluted freshly squeezed orange or lemon juice with honey is beneficial.

Craving a cigarette

Use a replacement strategy such as deep breathing, sipping on water or one of the many other replacement strategies you now have at your disposal.

Dry mouth

Stay hydrated by drinking lots of water. Sip on water or herbal tea throughout the day.

Fatigue

Deep breathing will give you more energy. Relaxation exercises will help you feel calm and energised. Rest when you need to rest. Providing you have no allergy, ginseng has been used to help combat fatigue, as has co-enzyme Q10. Check with your pharmacist or GP for advice.

Feelings of loss

Remember your reasons for stopping and remind yourself of what you are gaining. Repeat to yourself: 'This too shall pass.' Acceptance that cigarettes are gone from your life and that you are infinitely better off is the key to overcoming the feelings of loss.

Headache

Practise the Tortoise pose and work the acupressure points on the back of the hand as well as the eyebrow point.

Irritation, cranky feelings or anger

Hit a punching bag and let off some steam. Burn up the feelings with a fitness class. Practise the one-point or two-points meditation. Practise deep-breathing exercises. Repeat in your mind: 'Let it go.'

Insomnia

The key to a good night's sleep is to switch off your thinking and let go of physical tension. Avoid caffeine or other stimulants after midday every day. Avoid alcohol for several hours before going to bed. Burn up tension throughout the day by doing a minimum of 30 minutes' activity (i.e. walk, swim, cycle, gym).

Write lists for the next day's activities before going to bed. Avoid anxiety by keeping a 'worries journal' to get those thoughts out of your head and in a place where you can action them the next day.

Drink chamomile tea as a relaxant. Listen to soft music before preparing for bed. Avoid action-packed crime shows before bed. Avoid large meals late in the evening. Include snooze foods in your evening meal—these foods include low-fat dairy, soy products such as tofu, seafood, meats, poultry, whole grains, beans, hummus, lentils, eggs, sesame seeds and sunflower seeds.

Practise relaxation techniques and deep breathing.

Inability to concentrate

Include 'brain' foods such as apples, berries, carrots, green leafy vegetables, broccoli, fish, nuts, seeds, green tea and whole grains in your diet. Practise breathing exercises.

Mild depression

Reduce refined, starchy carbohydrates and high-sugar foods. Include in your diet lean meats, oats, spinach, bananas, nuts, wholegrain foods and a tablespoon of flaxseed oil every day. Introduce some fresh vegetable and apple juices into your day. Eat lots of salads. Practise relaxation techniques such as yoga, tai chi and chi kung, and get some sunshine. Taking vitamin B6 can also help.

Runny nose

Put eucalyptus drops in a bowl of steaming hot water and a towel over your head, then breathe the eucalyptus fumes in the steam.

Olbas oil, available from pharmacies, can be obtained in drop, lozenge or inhaler form. Put the drops on your pillow at night and rub it into your chest. Vicks Vapour Rub is also good to rub into your chest.

Sore throat

Lemon juice and honey in hot water with some fresh ginger crushed through a garlic crusher is an old favourite. Gargle with Condy's Crystals. Rub Vicks Vapour Rub into your throat and wrap a scarf around your throat. Propolis lozenges can help. Visualise you are in a snowfield and your hand is going into the snow. Imagine your hand becoming numb like an anaesthetic. Once you feel the tingly numb effect, place your hand over the affected area of your throat and let the numb feeling flow into your throat.

Sore tongue and/or gums

Avoid mouth washes unless they are natural. Drink plenty of water and warm tea. Avoid hot or cold foods. Eat soft foods. Clean your teeth after every meal. Check with your doctor or dentist if any of these symptoms persist.

Tightness in the chest

Rub Vicks Vapour Rub into your chest. Lie face down with your chest over the side of a bed or two pillows and have somebody drum all over your upper back with light fists. When I had a tight chest with asthma, this would really help loosen up the congestion. Be sure to have a tissue or spittoon handy.

Quitter's flu

Follow the steps listed above for a runny nose and sore throat.

PART III | Appendixes

APPENDIX 1: TOP 100 TIPS TO MAKE YOUR LIFE MORE COLOURFUL

1. Remember why you have decided to stop smoking. What are your reasons? Ask yourself whether your reasons for stopping smoking have changed.
2. Avoid situations in the first few weeks where you might be tempted.
3. Remind yourself you are now *smoke-free*. Change your focus and thoughts to something positive.
4. Listen to the bonus *Think Quit* sessions whenever the need arises.
5. Think about how healthy you can become.
6. Think about how much money you'll save.
7. Run on the spot.
8. See how many push-ups you can do.
9. Brush your teeth.
10. Floss your teeth.
11. Have a shower and scrub your body with a loofah.
12. Hire a treadmill and walk every night while watching TV.
13. Be prepared with activities that you will enjoy and that will help take your mind off the thought of smoking.
14. Join a yoga, tai chi or chi kung class.
15. Join a karate, ju jutsu or boxing class.
16. Go scuba diving.
17. Join a bushwalking club.

18. Volunteer at a shelter.
19. Volunteer at a hospital.
20. Make a mud puddle and squish your toes in it.
21. Make a foot rock massager. Get a plastic tray and fill it with small river pebbles, then fill with cool water and walk in it.
22. Stretch.
23. Meditate on a candle.
24. Meditate on a mantra. Make up your own mantra. It could be something calming like 'love and harmony' or something silly like 'eemo leeto lyto zonya'.
25. Visit a museum.
26. Book a dinner at a fancy restaurant.
27. Memorise the Quitline number: 131 848. They know what you are going through and can offer great advice and support.
28. Persuade a friend to join you and become a non-smoker.
29. Put *Smoke-Free Zone* notices or *No Smoking* logo stickers around you at work, at home and in your car.
30. Clean out your cupboards and drawers, disposing of everything you haven't worn or used for two years.
31. Clean out your garage.
32. Light some candles, play some music and take a hot bath.
33. Play your favourite music and dance naked around the house.
34. Play your favourite song and sing along as loudly as you can.
35. Sugar soap your walls.
36. Steam clean your carpets.
37. Wash your curtains.
38. Redecorate your house.
39. Make sure you have disposed of all memories that connect you to smoking, such as lighters, ashtrays and all the other paraphernalia. You may even like to smash ashtrays or take them to a rubbish bin far away from your home.

40. Be addicted … to health and fitness.
41. Have a siesta.
42. Wash the dog—or, if you don't have one, wash your neighbour's dog.
43. Listen to some relaxing music.
44. Keep substitutes like carrot sticks, celery sticks and apple pieces handy.
45. Chewing on ginger or cloves can also help you overcome a craving, as can sucking or chewing on cinnamon sticks.
46. Pumpkin seeds, sunflower seeds and chewing gum all help.
47. Brush your teeth several times a day with a soft toothbrush and get that fresh mint taste happening in your mouth.
48. Have your teeth cleaned by a dentist. Tell the dentist you have just stopped smoking and then enjoy the fresh taste in your mouth and how clean your teeth feel.
49. Take up a new hobby or take a craft or art class.
50. Learn origami from a book or online.
51. Take up poetry or creative writing.
52. Play marbles.
53. Play tennis or squash.
54. Visit church and pray.
55. Visit a Buddhist temple and meditate.
56. Visit an art gallery.
57. Hire a boat and go rowing.
58. Visit the zoo.
59. Visit a bird sanctuary.
60. Take up photography.
61. Learn to play the flute.
62. Take singing lessons.
63. Join Toastmasters and increase your confidence.
64. Make a big pot of vegetable soup and give half to the old lady down the street.

65. Make some cookies and share them with your neighbours.

66. Write a journal or diary of your escape from nicotine prison and subsequent freedom. Turn it into a book—who knows, it may be a bestseller! Be sure to mention *Think Quit*.

67. Avoid friends who are heavy smokers in the first few weeks.

68. Seek support from family and friends. Ask them to support and encourage you, especially in the first few weeks.

69. Exercise reduces stress and gives you energy. Make a plan to go bushwalking, or join classes or the gym, or go walking with a friend. There are a thousand things you could do.

70. Drink plenty of water to help flush out the nicotine and detoxify more quickly. Drink a minimum of 1 litre a day.

71. Sometimes cravings that go from one to three minutes seem longer because of what has been termed 'time distortion'. Keep a watch or clock handy and stay focused on something else.

72. Include a daily multi-vitamin. You may like to seek the advice of your pharmacist or doctor.

73. Cravings are the signal that the nicotine is leaving your system. Do the Zen thing and become one with the craving. Accept the craving for what it is and then change your focus. You could even say: 'Great! Another craving—the nicotine is leaving my system', and then put into practice one of your many habit-busting strategies. Remember, cravings are only temporary.

74. Drink fresh orange or cranberry juice.

75. Cravings, if they do happen, will last between one minute and three minutes. Rejoice and enthusiastically repeat to yourself: *This urge will pass. The nicotine is leaving my system. The new me is smoke-free.*

76. Have a hot or cold shower. The water running over your body can be very refreshing, and it is impossible to smoke while in the shower.

77. Read a book.

78. Read inspirational quotes online.
79. Join a forum and chat online.
80. Hand-paint a t-shirt.
81. Phone a friend you haven't spoken to for ages.
82. Ring someone and tell them how much they mean to you.
83. Watch a sunrise.
84. Watch a sunset.
85. Breathe fresh air.
86. Get a mini-trampoline and bounce on it.
87. Walk in a stream or by the water's edge at the beach.
88. If you are in your car, have your favourite band ready to go on CD then pump up the volume and sing along.
89. Drink herbal teas, including peppermint, lemongrass and chamomile. Chamomile is great to help you relax at night.
90. Take a thermos of herbal tea to work with you and sip on it throughout the day.
91. Remind yourself of all your reasons for quitting.
92. Go window shopping.
93. Write yourself a letter of encouragement and post it to yourself.
94. Read the White Pages telephone book. I'm serious—it is incredibly entertaining. Some of the names are rather unusual.
95. Watch a funny movie and laugh out loud.
96. Learn zone therapy and give yourself a foot massage.
97. Eat healthy, balanced meals and avoid going more than two or three hours without eating. This will help keep your blood sugar levels balanced. Under no circumstances should you skip a meal. Rather than eat more food, eat smaller, healthy meals more often.
98. If you feel stressed, anxious, upset or any negative emotion at all, take ten deep breaths and repeat your Think Quit mantra (see page 196).

99. Be prepared for the moments and times that you previously connected to smoking. Realise that every time you pass through the situation your resolve to be smoke-free becomes stronger and the connections become a distant memory, eventually disappearing altogether.

100. The most important top tip is yours. Write one down now.

APPENDIX 2: SEVEN-DAY SMOKING DIARY

Diary instructions

- You must record the number of the cigarette and the time you smoked it.
- Note what triggered or caused you to need the cigarette.
- Describe what you thought or felt before, during and after smoking each cigarette.
- After Day 1, note what replacement strategies you could use.

See the sample on page 234.

Time	Cig #	Trigger/reason	Feelings before	Feelings/thoughts after	Replacement strategies
7am	1	waking up	tired	more awake	Breathing exercise
8.am	2	drive to work	get moving	That's better	Sip water
9am	3	start work	excited	one day I'll quit	Power walk
9.30	4	on phone	automatic	Why did I do that	Breathing exercise
10.15	5	morn tea social	need to chat	I really need to stop	Eat carrot stick
11am	6	problem at work	stressed	Now I am relaxed	Resource anchor
12	7	success at work	need a reward	That feels better	Breathing exercise
12.30	8	finish...te	up ... meal	...stop	Drink...
2pm	9	then a...te	held... that	feel better	Sip water
3.15	10	tired	low and tired	still tired	Drink herbal tea
4pm	11	deadline break	pressure	more relaxed	Breathing exercise
5pm	12	walk to car	relieved day over	I didn't really need that	Sip water
5.20	13	driving	bored	it distracted me	Eat orange slice
5.45	14	driving	bored	That's better	Repeat affirmations
6.30	15	drinks at pub	be part of group	one day I'll quit	Breathing exercise
7pm	16	Drinks at pub	offered one	Why did I have that	Jog on spot
8pm	17	finish meal	will taste better	Hard to breathe	Chew gum
9 pm	18	drive home	lonely	smoking is disgusting	Breathing exercise
10pm	19	watch TV	bored	I know it's bad for me	Eat apple
10.30	20	before bed	what a day	gotta stop smoking	Sip water

SAMPLE

Day 1

Time	Cig #	Trigger	Feelings before	Feelings/thoughts after	Replacement strategies

Day 2

Time	Cig #	Trigger	Feelings before	Feelings/thoughts after	Replacement strategies

Day 3

Time	Cig #	Trigger	Feelings before	Feelings/thoughts after	Replacement strategies

Day 4

Time	Cig #	Trigger	Feelings before	Feelings/thoughts after	Replacement strategies

Day 5

Time	Cig #	Trigger	Feelings before	Feelings/thoughts after	Replacement strategies

Day 6

Time	Cig #	Trigger	Feelings before	Feelings/thoughts after	Replacement strategies

Day 7

Time	Cig #	Trigger	Feelings before	Feelings/thoughts after	Replacement strategies

Spare

Time	Cig #	Trigger	Feelings before	Feelings/thoughts after	Replacement strategies

Need extra support?

"You can do it on the spot. Instead of having a cigarette it's just a flick of the switch, put the earphones in, that's it, craving gone."

Pam Gill –
38 year smoker
Gold Coast

The Think Quit MP4 pocket therapist is your take-home hypnotherapist, mind coach and support person.

What you get:

✓ Pre-loaded MP4 player
✓ 12 hours of coaching/therapy
✓ 39 life changing audio sessions
✓ 23 video sessions
✓ 100 page Fast Action Success Manual

Bonus audio sessions include:
✓ 7 craving busting sessions
✓ Massive Motivation
✓ Alcohol Aversion
✓ Anti-Depression
✓ Think Sleep
✓ Feel Happy

Think Quit will be with you 24/7 to help you be smoke free and stay smoke free.

For a limited time receive the cost of this book or 10% which ever is greater off the R.R.P of $297. For more information or to order the program call 1300 76 00 73 or visit www.thinkquit.com.au. This offer is only valid within Australia and may be subject to change.

Take a break to break the habit

at Little Forest Health Retreat

Stop smoking weekend

Transform your life during a three-day weekend that will help you get on track and stay on track when it comes to being smoke free. Leave the stressors and triggers behind as you take care of the most important person in the world, you!

"The place is heaven on earth"
Jo Tregear - Victoria

Stop Smoking 7-Day retreat

Have a holiday, get healthy and stop smoking all at the same time. Spend seven days being guided through every step of the Think Quit program ensuring you know exactly how to stay smoke free forever.

"It was the best week of my life"
Pat France - Melbourne

5-Day Detox

Enjoy five days of organic juices, healing teas, healthy meals, daily Tai Chi and self-healing hypnosis sessions as you cleanse, rejuvenate and transform your mind and body. Give your body a break and jump-start your health.

"The food at the retreat was amazing"
Rob Gourlay - Victoria

Inner-makeover weekend

Tranquility, rejuvenation and self-healing are the main focus of this two-day weekend workshop. Relax more deeply than you ever thought possible while activating your bodys' own internal healer.

"Absolutely life changing, I wish it lasted longer,"
Sue Jackson - QLD

Think Slim weekend

This three-day weekend will help you overcome the mental challenges that may be weighing you down. Eat healthy, get fit and focus on your goal.

"The way Mark gets to the cause of the problem is magic"
Rebecca Bailey QLD

Think Slim 7-Day retreat

Most weight loss retreats around the world focus on diet and exercise. A large part of your time spent at Little Forest will be helping you unload the emotional baggage. You will be supported to change the way you think about food, activity and yourself.

"It's paradise"
Susan Savage Melbourne

Note: All Little Forest weekends and retreats include accommodation, healthy organic meals, daily workouts, workshops and hypnosis sessions. For more information, rates or to book a retreat call 1300 76 00 73 or visit www.innermakeover.com.au .

Key Concerns in Media Studies

Series Editor: Andrew Crisell

Within the context of today's global, digital environment, *Key Concerns in Media Studies* addresses themes and concepts that are integral to the study of media. Concisely written by leading academics, the books consider the historical development of these themes and the theories that underpin them, and assess their overall significance, using up-to-date examples and case studies throughout. By giving a clear overview of each topic, the series provides an ideal starting point for all students of modern media.

Published

Forthcoming

Gender in the Media